How to Use Your Snap Revision Text Guide

his *Much Ado About Nothing* Snap Revisio    ark
n your AQA English Literature exam. It is di   can
asily find help for the bits you find tricky. T   ed
o know for the exam:

lot: what happens in the play?

etting and Context: what periods, places, e . ____
nderstanding the play?

haracters: who are the main characters, how are they presented, and how do
hey change?

hemes: what ideas does the author explore in the play, and how are they shown?

he Exam: what kinds of question will come up in your exam, and how can you
et top marks?

o help you get ready for your exam, each two-page topic includes the following:

Key Quotations to Learn

hort quotations to memorise that will allow you to analyse in the exam and boost
our grade.

Summary

 recap of the most important points covered in the topic.

Sample Analysis

n example of the kind of analysis that the examiner will be looking for.

Quick Test

 quick-fire test to check you can remember the main points from the topic.

Exam Practice

 short writing task so you can practise applying what you've covered in the topic.

Glossary

 handy list of words you will find useful when revising *Much Ado About Nothing*
with easy-to-understand definitions.

AUTHOR:

IAN
KIRBY

 ebook

To access the ebook version of this
Snap Revision Text Guide, visit

collins.co.uk/ebooks

and follow the step-by-step instructions.

Published by Collins
An imprint of HarperCollins*Publishers*
1 London Bridge Street
London SE1 9GF

HarperCollins*Publishers*
1st Floor, Watermarque Building,
Ringsend Road, Dublin 4, Ireland

© HarperCollins*Publishers* Limited 2022

ISBN 978-0-00-852033-5

First published 2022

10 9 8 7 6 5 4 3 2 1

British Library Cataloguing in Publication Data.

A CIP record of this book is available from the
British Library.

Commissioning Editor: Claire Souza
Project managers: Fiona Watson and
Shelley Teasdale
Author: Ian Kirby
Copy editor: Fiona Watson
Proofreader: Frances Cooper
Reviewer: Shelley Welsh
Typesetting: Q2A Media
Cover designers: Kneath Associates and
Sarah Duxbury
Production: Karen Nulty
Printed and bound in the UK using 100% Renewable Electricity at CPI Group (UK) Ltd

ACKNOWLEDGEMENTS
The author and publisher are grateful to
the copyright holders for permission to use
quoted materials and images.
Every effort has been made to trace copyright
holders and obtain their permission for the
use of copyright material. The author and
publisher will gladly receive information
enabling them to rectify any error or omission
in subsequent editions. All facts are correct at
time of going to press.

MIX
Paper from
responsible source

FSC
www.fsc.org   **FSC™ C007454**

This book is produced from independently
certified FSC™ paper to ensure responsible
forest management.

For more information visit:
www.harpercollins.co.uk/green

Contents

Act 1 scene 1

You must be able to: understand what happens in the first scene of Act 1.

Lines 1–87

A messenger has reported to Leonato that Don Pedro, the Prince, is due to arrive at Messina with his soldiers. He adds that 'Don Pedro hath bestowed much honour' on a young man, Count Claudio, who has fought particularly well in the wars.

Beatrice asks if Benedick has returned from the wars. She refers to him mockingly as 'Signior Mountanto', using the word for a fencer or duellist to introduce how the two of them are always in conflict.

The Messenger and Leonato try to stand up for Benedick, 'you tax Signior Benedick too much', but Beatrice continues to mock him, adding that she feels sorry for Claudio being his friend.

Lines 88–149

Don Pedro arrives and Leonato greets him, saying he is always a trouble-free guest.

Benedick makes a playful joke that Leonato may not be Hero's father and Leonato makes a witty riposte that implies Benedick is a womaniser.

As Leonato and Don Pedro move off together, Benedick keeps talking. This prompts Beatrice to mock him: 'I wonder that you will still be talking, Signior Benedick: nobody marks you.' The pair begin to quarrel, using insults, **repetition** and **wordplay**.

Don Pedro announces his plan to stay for at least a month. After showing his happiness that Don John has **reconciled** with his brother, Don Pedro, Leonato leads everyone into the house.

Lines 150–308

Benedick and Claudio remain. Claudio reveals his attraction to Hero, 'she is the sweetest lady that ever I looked on', but Benedick playfully dismisses it and tries to dissuade him from any plans to 'turn husband'.

Don Pedro returns and Benedick shares his dismay at Claudio falling in love. Don Pedro is more supportive of the match: 'Amen, if you love her, for the lady is very well worthy.'

Don Pedro mocks Benedick's attitude to marriage and predicts he will fall in love one day.

After Benedick leaves, Claudio describes his passion for Hero. Don Pedro wants to help to secure the relationship. As there is due to be a masked party in the evening, he suggests that he pretends to be Claudio and **woos** Hero.

Key Quotations to Learn

Beatrice: 'God help the noble Claudio! If he have caught the Benedick, it will cost him a thousand pound ere a' be cured.'

Leonato: 'Never came trouble to my house in the likeness of your Grace.'

Benedick: 'What, my dear Lady Disdain! Are you yet living?'

Summary

The first scene introduces Leonato's family and Don Pedro's army.

There is witty tension between Beatrice and Benedick.

Claudio is introduced as an honourable young man who quickly falls in love with Hero.

Benedick tries to diminish Claudio's feelings but Don Pedro encourages him.

Don Pedro outlines his plan to woo Hero for Claudio by disguising himself as the young lover.

Questions

QUICK TEST

- Why is Don Pedro pleased with Claudio?
- Beatrice and Benedick quarrel in the first scene. Who begins the quarrel?
- What recent change has taken place in the relationship between Don Pedro and his brother, Don John?
- How do Don Pedro and Benedick react differently to Claudio falling in love with Hero?

EXAM PRACTICE

Using one or more of the 'Key Quotations to Learn', write a paragraph analysing how the comic feud between Beatrice and Benedick is presented in the opening scene.

Act 1 scenes 2 and 3

You must be able to: understand what happens in the second half of Act 1.

Act 1 scene 2

Leonato meets with his brother, Antonio.

A servant of Antonio's has – mistakenly – overheard Don Pedro telling Claudio that he is in love with Hero and plans to woo her in the evening. This creates **dramatic irony** as the audience know that it is in fact Claudio who loves Hero and that Don Pedro is going to pretend to be Claudio to woo her for him.

Leonato is doubtful of the story but Antonio reassures him that the servant is 'a good sharp fellow'.

Despite deciding not to believe the story until it is a reality, 'we will hold it as a dream till it appear itself', Leonato asks Antonio to tell Hero so she can be prepared to give her response.

Act 1 scene 3

Don John is talking to Conrade. He explains his unhappiness, linking it to his **illegitimacy**, and says he refuses to change his attitudes or behaviour to suit others. Conrade encourages him to be more positive in front of his brother, Don Pedro, in order to improve his social position: 'It is needful that you frame the season for your own harvest.'

Don John calls himself a 'villain' and, again, relates it to his illegitimate status: he feels trapped, 'in my cage', by the need to stay on good terms with his brother, the legitimate prince.

Borachio enters and reveals that someone is due to get married. Don John states his dislike of marriage, calling it 'unquietness', and hopes to cause some 'mischief'.

Borachio explains that Claudio is in love with Hero. Don John's dislike of Claudio is apparent through his **ironic** description of him as 'exquisite' and the insult 'a very forward March-chick' (suggesting that Claudio is **presumptuous** to love the daughter of someone with as much social status as Leonato). He later complains that he should have Claudio's position as right-hand man to Don Pedro: 'that young start-up hath all the glory of my overthrow.'

When Borachio reveals how Don Pedro will woo Hero on Claudio's behalf, Don John enlists his friends to help him ruin the plan.

Key Quotations to Learn

Don John: 'I cannot hide what I am: I must be sad when I have cause and smile at no man's jests …' (Iiii)

Don John: 'If I had my mouth, I would bite; if I had my liberty, I would do my liking.' (Iiii)

Don John: 'What is he for a fool that betroths himself to unquietness?' (Iiii)

Summary

- Antonio leads Leonato to believe, mistakenly, that Don Pedro is in love with Hero.
- Don John is introduced as an unhappy, unsociable and destructive person.
- Don John resents his illegitimate status, showing particular dislike towards his brother, Don Pedro, and Claudio.
- Together with Borachio and Conrade, Don Jon plans to ruin Don Pedro's plan to woo Hero for Claudio.

Questions

QUICK TEST
1.   How does Shakespeare create dramatic irony in Act 1 scene 2?
2.   Why doesn't Don John have the same status as his brother, Don Pedro?
3.   What is Don John's attitude towards Claudio?
4.   What is Don John's view of marriage?

EXAM PRACTICE
Using one or more of the 'Key Quotations to Learn', write a paragraph analysing how Don John is presented in Act 1.

Act 2 scene 1

You must be able to: understand what happens in Act 2 scene 1.

Lines 1–75
Beatrice and Hero discuss the impression they have of Don John as unhappy and unfriendly. Beatrice turns their discussion into another criticism of Benedick.

Leonato and Antonio joke with Beatrice about her attitude to men. She says she feels blessed not to be bothered with a husband and that no man is right for her.

Antonio tells Hero that he hopes she will follow Leonato's guidance in marriage (believing that she is about to be wooed by Don Pedro). Leonato reminds Hero that she knows what to say (the implication is that she will agree) should Don Pedro woo her. However, Beatrice warns her against marriage, saying it always ends in regret, 'then comes repentance'.

Lines 76–144
Don Pedro and his men arrive, masked, for the dance. He begins to woo Hero and part of their conversation is presented by Shakespeare as a **quatrain** of poetry ('My visor is Philemon's roof …') to create the idea of romance.

Benedick, masked, has tried to annoy Beatrice by relating how another man told him she was 'disdainful'. However, the joke rebounds on Benedick when she tells the apparent stranger that it was probably Benedick who criticised her, then goes on to describe him as 'the Prince's jester, a very dull fool'.

Lines 145–365
Don John and Borachio notice Claudio. When Claudio approaches them, he pretends to be Benedick. They claim that they have heard Don Pedro 'swear his affection' for Hero, and want to dissuade him because she is not of equal social status.

Upset, Claudio thinks Don Pedro has betrayed him and believes he has lost his chance with Hero.

Benedick meets with Claudio, telling him that Don Pedro has wooed Hero on his behalf, but Claudio does not believe him and leaves angrily. Left alone, Benedick's short **soliloquy** reveals how he was hurt by Beatrice's opinion of him.

Don Pedro returns with Hero and Leonato. Benedick explains that Claudio thinks the Prince has wooed Hero for himself. Don Pedro aims to repair the situation.

Benedick explains how Beatrice has offended him and, when she reappears with Claudio, he leaves.

Claudio is pleased to discover that Hero will be his wife and that Don Pedro has not betrayed him.

Don Pedro and Beatrice joke together about marriage. He is impressed by her happy nature and, after she leaves, plans with Leonato, Hero and Claudio to bring Beatrice and Benedick together.

Key Quotations to Learn

Claudio: 'Friendship is constant in all other things / Save in the office and affairs of love.'

Claudio: 'Lady, as you are mine, I am yours; I give away myself for you and dote upon the exchange.'

Don Pedro: 'I will undertake ... one of Hercules' labours, which is to bring Signior Benedick and the Lady Beatrice into a mountain of affection ...'

Summary

- At the dance, Leonato readies Hero to accept Don Pedro's proposal.
- Benedick tries to annoy Beatrice but ends up being upset by her opinion of him.
- Don Pedro woos Hero for Claudio. However, Don John and Borachio tell Claudio that Don Pedro is wooing her for himself.
- Claudio has not been betrayed by Don Pedro; he and Hero are to be married.
- Don Pedro plans to unite Beatrice and Benedick in love.

Questions

QUICK TEST
1. What do Beatrice and Hero think of Don John?
2. What is Leonato expecting to happen at the dance?
3. What upsets Benedick?
4. How does Claudio react when he thinks Don Pedro has wooed Hero for himself?

EXAM PRACTICE
Using one or more of the 'Key Quotations to Learn', write a paragraph analysing how love is presented in Act 2.

Act 2 scenes 2 and 3

You must be able to: understand what happens in the second half of Act 2.

Act 2 scene 2

Don John is unhappy that Claudio is happy and wants 'to be the death of this marriage'.

Borachio assures him that he can still 'cross' the marriage. He tells Don John to go to Don Pedro, pretending that he respects his brother and Claudio. He should tell them that Hero is actually in love with Borachio. To provide evidence, Borachio plans to speak to Margaret (Hero's lady-in-waiting) at the window of Hero's chamber as if she is Hero; when Don Pedro and Claudio witness the encounter they will think Hero is unfaithful.

Borachio describes how this will 'misuse the Prince, to vex Claudio, to undo Hero, and kill Leonato'.

Don John offers to reward Borachio with a thousand ducats for his cunning.

Act 2 scene 3

Benedick gives a soliloquy on love. He wonders how Claudio, who has previously mocked others for falling in love, can himself have fallen in love. He is surprised that this great soldier has now become a romantic.

He wonders whether he could experience the same change. He cannot imagine falling in love and lists the many different qualities a woman would need: beauty, wisdom, grace, virtue, wealth, mildness, nobility, good at speaking, musical … but any colour hair.

As Don Pedro, Claudio and Leonato approach, Benedick hides himself in the garden. They see him but pretend that they haven't.

Together, the men discuss how much Beatrice is in love with Benedick, claiming that she feels an 'enraged affection' but is unable to admit her feelings to Benedick. Leonato says Hero has told him that Beatrice will sit up all night, trying to write to Benedick about her love.

Shakespeare uses **asides** to show Benedick's interest and Claudio's encouragement of the prank.

The men continue to talk about Beatrice's sweetness, virtue and wisdom before showing sympathy for her lovesickness. They praise Benedick but say it is pointless to tell him of Beatrice's love.

The pretence over, the men leave and Benedick emerges. He admits his love in a soliloquy. When Beatrice approaches to tell him that it is time for dinner, he twists the meaning of her words to convince himself that she loves him.

Key Quotations to Learn

Benedick: '... man is a fool when he dedicates his behaviours to love ...' (IIiii)

Benedick: '... I have railed so long against marriage: but doth not the appetite alter?' (IIiii)

Benedick: 'When I said I would die a bachelor, I did not think I should live till I were married.' (IIiii)

Summary

- Don John and Borachio plan to destroy Claudio and Hero's happiness.
- Benedick is surprised by how Claudio has changed from a soldier to a romantic.
- Don Pedro, Claudio and Leonato (knowing they are being overheard by Benedick) pretend that Hero has told them how much Beatrice is in love with Benedick.
- Benedick privately admits his love for Beatrice.

Questions

QUICK TEST
1. What is Borachio's plan?
2. Why is Benedick surprised that Claudio has fallen in love?
3. What do Leonato, Don Pedro and Claudio claim is the reason Beatrice speaks so harshly to Benedick?
4. What does Benedick realise about himself by the end of Act 2?

EXAM PRACTICE
Using one or more of the 'Key Quotations to Learn', write a paragraph analysing how Benedick is presented as changing in Act 2.

Act 3 scenes 1 and 2

You must be able to: understand what happens in the first half of Act 3.

Act 3 scene 1

Mirroring the previous scene, Hero, Margaret and Ursula get ready to fool Beatrice into falling in love with Benedick.

Beatrice enters the garden and listens to Hero and Ursula's conversation. Again, Shakespeare uses dramatic irony to create comedy as the audience knows that Beatrice is being tricked.

Hero reports that Don Pedro and Claudio have told her that Benedick is in love with Beatrice. She adds that she instructed them not to tell Beatrice because she is 'self-endeared' and cannot love anyone. Ursula agrees that Beatrice would only use the knowledge to mock ('make sport' with) Benedick.

Just as Don Pedro and Claudio described Beatrice's qualities in the previous scene, Hero describes Benedick as wise, young and noble. However, she says that Beatrice would only find fault with all of his qualities. Because of this, Hero says she will not tell Beatrice about Benedick's love. Instead she will advise Benedick to 'fight against his passion'. She adds that he is second only to Claudio in the whole of Italy, and Ursula agrees.

After they leave, like Benedick, Beatrice delivers a soliloquy. She is upset to hear that others think her full of 'pride and scorn' and decides to return ('requite') Benedick's love.

Act 3 scene 2

Don Pedro, Claudio and Leonato discuss Benedick's recent change in behaviour. Knowing he is thinking about Beatrice, they suggest he is lovesick. However, wanting to hide the truth, Benedick claims he has toothache.

Benedick asks to speak to Leonato in private. Left alone, Don Pedro and Claudio speculate that Benedick is going to tell Leonato his feelings for Beatrice.

Don John arrives and says that Claudio may not wish to marry Hero 'when he knows what I know'. Following his and Borachio's plan, Don John explains that Hero is 'disloyal' and that he will show them evidence at midnight.

Claudio announces that if it is true about her **infidelity**, he will 'shame her' in front of everyone at the wedding. As he took part in the wooing, Don Pedro says that he will also 'join with thee to disgrace her'.

Hero: 'Then go we near her, that her ear lose nothing / Of the false sweet bait that we lay for it.' (IIIi)

Hero: 'Therefore let Benedick, like cover'd fire, / Consume away in sighs, waste inwardly.' (IIIi)

Don John: 'O plague right well prevented!' (IIIii)

Summary

Act 3 scene 1 mirrors Act 2 scene 3 but focuses on the tricking of Beatrice.

Hero and Ursula discuss Benedick's love for Beatrice, knowing she can hear them.

They criticise Beatrice's unloving attitude and, once they leave, she decides to return Benedick's love.

Don Pedro, Claudio and Leonato joke that Benedick is lovesick but he pretends to have toothache.

Don John brings news to Don Pedro and Claudio that Hero is unfaithful.

Questions

QUICK TEST

1. What dramatic technique is Shakespeare using when the audience knows that Beatrice is being tricked but she is unaware?
2. What reasons do Ursula and Hero give for not telling Beatrice that Benedick is in love with her?
3. What do Don Pedro and Claudio think is the reason for Benedick wanting to speak to Leonato in private?
4. What do Claudio and Don Pedro plan to do if Don John's information about Hero's unfaithfulness is proven to be true?

EXAM PRACTICE

Using one or more of the 'Key Quotations to Learn', write a paragraph analysing how deception is presented in Act 3.

You must be able to: understand what happens in the second half of Act 3.

Act 3 scene 3

Dogberry, the constable, is talking to Verges and the two watchmen about their responsibilities. Shakespeare creates comedy through Dogberry's **malapropisms**. He often misuses words, giving the opposite meaning to what he intends. For example, he praises the second watchman for being 'the most senseless' (instead of sensible) person for the job, then tells the men that they should not make a lot of noise as it would be 'most tolerable' (instead of intolerable).

Dogberry and Verges exit as Borachio and Conrade appear, not realising that they are observed by the two watchmen.

Borachio drunkenly boasts of how Don John has paid him a thousand ducats. He talks about how clothes can hide what a person is really like before revealing how he has wooed Margaret as if she was Hero. He adds how Don John made sure that Claudio and Don Pedro were watching, and that Claudio left 'enraged' and ready to shame Hero at the wedding the following day.

Having heard Borachio's tale, the watchmen detain Borachio and Conrade.

Act 3 scene 4

Shakespeare creates dramatic irony again as Hero is seen preparing for the wedding ceremony, unaware of the previous night's events.

An **ominous** tone is created when Hero feels something is wrong: 'my heart is exceeding heavy'. However, Margaret turns this into a **bawdy** joke about Hero soon feeling 'the weight of a man'.

Beatrice arrives, trying to hide her lovesickness by claiming that she has a cold. She and Margaret exchange witty retorts.

Hero and Margaret make jokes that suggest Beatrice is in love, such as suggesting she cure herself with some 'carduus benedictus' (a well-known medicinal plant and a play on words as the name is similar to 'Benedick').

Act 3 scene 5

Dogberry and Verges arrive to speak to Leonato, despite him being busy with his daughter's impending marriage. Again, comedy is created through Dogberry's malapropisms, such as 'Comparisons are odorous' (he means odious), and Leonato's witty responses.

With Dogberry failing to fully explain the arrest of Borachio and Conrade, and Leonato too busy to examine them further, the truth is not yet revealed. Instead, Leonato commands Dogberry and Verges to question the men and bring him the details later.

Key Quotations to Learn

Margaret: 'A maid, and stuffed! There's goodly catching of cold.' (IIIiv)

Margaret: 'Doth not my wit become me rarely?' / Beatrice: 'It is not seen enough, you should wear it in your cap.' (IIIiv)

Dogberry: 'One word, sir: our watch, sir, have indeed comprehended two aspicious persons …' (IIIv)

Summary

- Shakespeare introduces the comic characters of Dogberry and the watchmen. They are presented as lacking intelligence by regularly using words with the opposite meaning to what they intend.
- Borachio tells Conrade of how he and Don John have deceived Claudio and Don Pedro. They are arrested by the watchmen.
- Prior to the wedding, Hero, Margaret and Beatrice make jokes (mostly at Beatrice's expense) about love.
- Dogberry and Verges try to report the arrest of Borachio and Conrade to Leonato. However, they come across as foolish and Leonato is too busy to listen.

Questions

QUICK TEST
1. What is the key comic characteristic of Dogberry's speech?
2. Who have deceived Claudio and Don Pedro?
3. How does Beatrice try to hide that she is feeling sick with love for Benedick?
4. Despite being excited about her wedding day, what other tone is used when Hero speaks?

EXAM PRACTICE
Using one or more of the 'Key Quotations to Learn', write a paragraph analysing how humour is created in Act 3.

You must be able to: understand what happens in Act 4.

Act 4 scene 1

At the wedding ceremony, Claudio is rude to Hero and says he will not marry her. At first, Leonato and Benedick think he is joking.

Claudio then calls her unfaithful, 'Give not this rotten orange to your friend; / She's but the sign and semblance of her honour', claiming that she only pretends to be virtuous. He uses a **simile** sarcastically, 'how like a maid she blushes', to further accuse her of being unfaithful.

Leonato is shocked and initially thinks that Claudio is admitting to having slept with Hero before the marriage but he denies this.

Hero is also shocked, 'Is my lord well that he doth speak so wide?', but Don Pedro support Claudio and calls her a 'stale', suggesting she is **promiscuous** or a prostitute.

Don Pedro reports what they saw the previous evening. Hero tries to defend herself, 'I talk'd with no man at that hour, my lord', but Don John confirms the accusations.

Hero faints and Leonato, thinking she is dead, harshly says: 'Death is the fairest cover for her shame'.

Don Pedro's men leave but Benedick stays behind. After Leonato describes his disappointment in Hero and his wish for her to die, Benedick joins Beatrice and the Friar in trying to defend Hero from Claudio's claims. They think there has been a mistake ('my cousin is belied') but Leonato will not listen.

Regaining consciousness, Hero begs her father to believe her while Benedick suspects a plot by Don John: 'the practice of it lives in John the bastard'. Leonato begins to be swayed: he says that if Hero has lied, his 'hands shall tear her' but if Claudio and Don Pedr are proven wrong, he will have them murdered.

The Friar suggests pretending that Hero has died in order to 'change slander to remorse', in the hope that Claudio will regret his actions.

Left alone, Beatrice and Benedick worry about Hero and admit their love for each other. Beatrice asks him to kill Claudio. At first he refuses but she says he would do it if he truly loved her; reluctantly, Benedick agrees to challenge Claudio to a **duel**.

Act 4 scene 2

In a more comic scene, Dogberry and his watchmen bring Borachio and Conrade to be questioned in front of the local Sexton.

It is reported that Hero has died and that Don John has vanished.

The Sexton orders the suspects to be brought before Leonato.

Key Quotations to Learn

Claudio: 'She knows the heat of a luxurious bed; / Her blush is guiltiness, not modesty.' (IVi)

Leonato: 'O, she is fall'n / Into a pit of ink, that the wide sea / Hath drops too few to wash her clean again ...' (IVi)

Benedick: 'By this hand I love thee.' / Beatrice: 'Use it for my love some other way than swearing by it.' (IVi)

Friar: '... If this sweet lady lie not guiltless here / Under some biting error.' (IVi)

Summary

- At the wedding, Claudio refuses to marry Hero and accuses her of being unfaithful. His claims are supported by Don Pedro and Don John.

- Leonato and Hero are shocked. Leonato is so ashamed that, when she faints, he hopes she is dead.

- Benedick, Beatrice and the Friar believe Hero. The Friar suggests they announce that Hero has died, hoping that Claudio will regret his behaviour.

- Benedick and Beatrice admit their love for each other and she convinces him to kill Claudio as a sign of his love for her.

Questions

QUICK TEST
1. How do people initially react to Claudio refusing to marry Hero?
2. How does Leonato react when he thinks Hero has died?
3. Why does he react in this way?
4. How does Beatrice convince Benedick to challenge Claudio to a duel?

EXAM PRACTICE
Using one or more of the 'Key Quotations to Learn', write a paragraph analysing how Shakespeare presents characters' attitudes towards Hero in Act 4.

You must be able to: understand what happens in Act 5.

Act 5 scene 1

Leonato tells his brother, Antonio, that no one can understand the depth of his grief. He has come to believe Hero: 'My soul doth tell me Hero is belied'. He wants Claudio and Don Pedro to suffer for their actions, at which point they enter the scene (believing that Hero has died).

Leonato accuses Claudio of having 'wrong'd mine innocent child and me'. He and Antonio both challenge Claudio to duels. Antonio criticises Claudio and Don Pedro as 'Scambling, outfacing, fashion-monging boys, / That lie and cog and flout, deprave and slander'.

Don Pedro continues to support Claudio so Leonato and Antonio leave. Benedick arrives and Don Pedro and Claudio say they have been looking for him to cheer them up ('Wilt thou use thy wit?'). Benedick calls Claudio 'a villain' and challenges him to a duel. Don Pedro and Claudio try to joke with Benedick but he is resolute and leaves.

Dogberry and the watchmen arrive with Borachio and Conrade. Don Pedro and Claudio are shocked when Borachio confesses his part in Don John's treachery. Leonato arrives, hears Borachio's confession and asserts that Don Pedro and Claudio are equally guilty. The two men offer to do any 'penance' to make amends. Leonato pretends he has a niece who looks like Hero; he says Claudio must marry her the following morning.

Act 5 scene 2

Benedick tells Margaret that he wishes to speak to Beatrice. While waiting, he describes his difficulty in expressing his love. Beatrice arrives and is initially angry that Benedick has not killed Claudio but he assures her that he has challenged him to a duel. They talk of the strangeness of their quarrelsome love. Ursula arrives with news that the truth has been uncovered.

Act 5 scene 3

At Hero's tomb, Claudio reads an **epitaph**, regretting how she was 'Done to death by slanderous tongues'. He pledges to perform the **rite** every year.

Act 5 scene 4

Talking to the Friar, Leonato acknowledges that Claudio and Don Pedro were also innocent victims of Don John. Benedick asks Leonato if he may marry Beatrice; he agrees.

Don Pedro and Claudio arrive. The women enter, masked, and Claudio marries who he believes to be Antonio's daughter. Once the ceremony is complete, Hero removes her mask and Leonato admits to Claudio that Hero only 'died, my lord, but while her slander liv'd'.

Beatrice also unmasks. At first, neither she nor Benedick will admit their love and they realise they have been tricked by their friends. However, Claudio and Hero reveal love

nnets Beatrice and Benedick have written about each other. The pair kiss, jokingly
dmit their love, and plan to marry. A messenger brings news that Don John has been
prehended, and the play ends with a dance.

Key Quotations to Learn

Leonato: 'Bring me a father that so lov'd his child, / Whose joy of her is overwhelm'd like mine.' (Vi)

Antonio: 'God knows I lov'd my niece, / And she is dead, slander'd to death by villains …' (Vi)

Don Pedro: 'Runs not this speech like iron through your blood?' / Claudio: 'I have drunk poison whiles he utter'd it.' (Vi)

Benedick: 'Here's our own hands against our hearts. Come, I will have thee, but by this light I take thee for pity' / Beatrice: '… I yield upon great persuasion, and partly to save your life, for I was told you were in a consumption.' (Viv)

Summary

- Leonato and Antonio are angry with Don Pedro and Claudio but they still maintain their accusation against Hero.
- Benedick challenges Claudio to a duel.
- Borachio confesses his crimes. Don Pedro and Claudio are shocked. Leonato says that, to make amends, Claudio must now marry his niece.
- After the wedding, the niece is revealed to be Hero.
- Benedick and Beatrice realise that they have been tricked into love by their friends. Still joking with each other, they agree to marry.

Questions

QUICK TEST
1. How has Leonato's view of Hero changed since Act 4?
2. How do Don Pedro and Claudio react when Don John's plot is revealed?
3. Who does Claudio believe he is marrying at the end of the play?
4. What proof of Beatrice and Benedick's love is finally revealed?

EXAM PRACTICE
Using one or more of the 'Key Quotations to Learn', write a paragraph analysing how powerful emotions are presented in Act 5.

16th-century Messina, Sicily

You must be able to: understand how the play relates to its setting.

What is the play's setting?

Much Ado About Nothing is based in Messina, an old city on the Mediterranean island of Sicily (which is now part of Italy). The play is based in the 16th century when Messina was a very important trading port; there had been several wars because people wanted to control it.

The climate would have been warm and sunny – very different to what Shakespeare's English audience were mostly used to. His choice of a Mediterranean setting helps him to create a sense of **escapism** with an atmosphere of romance and comedy. On the whole, the characters seem very relaxed and happily swap jokes with each other that – in other contexts – could be offensive (such as Benedick's wholly humorous suggestion in Act 1 scene 1 that Hero might not actually be Leonato's daughter).

We are mostly presented with rich, privileged characters with few problems, which would also have added to the escapism for much of Shakespeare's audience.

How are gender roles significant to the context?

Despite the bright atmosphere that matches the setting, *Much Ado About Nothing* presents a society of which modern readers might disapprove. The social structure is clearly **patriarchal**, meaning that men hold all the power. Most of the important characters are male and the majority of the female characters are submissive to men, especially Hero who is almost silent in the early scenes. Even Beatrice, who is a strong and witty character, needs Benedick to avenge Hero on her behalf and ends the play with a more **conventional** role through marriage.

However, it is important to remember that, when the play was first performed, Shakespeare's audience would have seen this as normal. Beatrice's forthright behaviour and the way she speaks to the men as if she is their equal would have been enjoyably surprising. Similarly, Hero would have matched their expectations of a romantic heroine.

How was marriage different to today?

The way in which Hero is courted – with Leonato and Antonio expecting Hero to follow their instructions about who to marry, and Leonato's parental permission being sought – may seem a little unusual to a modern audience.

In the 16th century, especially amongst wealthy families, marriage was seen as a way to extend status, and love wasn't necessarily the main concern. It was also very important to ask a father's permission for marriage. Hero is presented as marrying into a similar class (Claudio is a Count) so there are no objections to the marriage.

Because men held most of the wealth and power in society, it was unusual for a woman not to get married. For most women, marriage was an economic necessity as much as a social expectation. Coming from a wealthy family, Beatrice perhaps has the privilege of not *needing* to marry.

ferent attitudes at the time meant that there were different expectations of male and
ale behaviour. Whilst a married woman would have to display complete faithfulness, it
s generally accepted that a wealthy man might have a mistress as well as his wife, often
ding to an illegitimate child. That child, especially if a boy, would often be brought
in the married household and would have privileges as the child of a wealthy man.
wever, they would not have the same status or legal rights as a legitimate child and
uld always be known as a 'bastard' (Don John).

Summary

The play is set in the Mediterranean port city of Messina in the 16th century.

The sunny setting helps Shakespeare to create a romantic and comic atmosphere,
allowing his English audience some escapism.

The characters are mostly wealthy and care-free, adding to the sense of escapism.

For a modern audience, the social structure appears old-fashioned and patriarchal.
This affects the way in which gender and marriage are presented.

Questions

UICK TEST

. Why might Shakespeare have chosen a Mediterranean setting?
. In what way is Hero a conventional 16th-century female character?
. In what way is Beatrice an unconventional 16th-century female character?
. Why is Don John referred to as a 'bastard'?

XAM PRACTICE

Act 2 scene 1, Shakespeare presents different attitudes to marriage.

NTONIO [To HERO] Well, niece, I trust you will be ruled by your father.

EATRICE Yes, faith, it is my cousin's duty to make curtsy and say 'Father, as it please
you.' But yet for all that, cousin, let him be a handsome fellow, or else
make another curtsy and say 'Father, as it please me.'

EONATO Well, niece, I hope to see you one day fitted with a husband.

EATRICE Not till God make men of some other metal than earth. Would it not grieve
a woman to be overmastered with a piece of valiant dust? To make an
account of her life to a clod of wayward marl? No, uncle, I'll none: Adam's
sons are my brethren; and, truly, I hold it a sin to match in my kindred.

EONATO [To HERO] Daughter, remember what I told you: if the prince do solicit you
in that kind, you know your answer.

Vrite a paragraph explaining how the characters' different attitudes to marriage relate
o the 16th-century context.

You must be able to: understand how the play reflects the time in which it was written.

When was the play written?

Inspired by several European love stories, *Much Ado About Nothing* is believed to have been written between 1598 and 1599. The play was very popular and performed regularly.

How does the play reflect Elizabethan England?

The presentation of social hierarchies, expectations of gender roles and the importance of marriage would have matched the lives of Shakespeare's initial audience: they looked up to people of a higher class, saw men as more important than women and thought women should marry and take on a domestic role in life.

These aspects of society are explored and sometimes **subverted** by Shakespeare, such as in the criticisms of marriage, Beatrice's strength and independence, and men of high status being fooled into errors of judgement. However, by the end, the audience's conventional expectations of society are restored. It can be argued that this allows the play to present slightly radical or progressive social ideas within a safe scenario.

In Shakespeare's time, the word's 'nothing' and 'noting' sounded similar. He uses this **pun** to suggest that the play is all about how people observe and gossip about others (noting), creating judgements and consequences that are actually false or baseless (nothing). Such behaviour was as prevalent in the Elizabethan age as it is today.

Characters like Don Pedro and Claudio also display the **courtly** behaviour, alongside ideas of honour and shame, that was expected amongst the higher classes at the time.

The previous century had seen the Wars of the Roses, a turbulent period of power struggles that was recent history to Shakespeare's audience. Although kept in the background of the play, the arrival of Don Pedro's army from the war alludes to these ideas of conflict. Similarly, Don Pedro's relationship with his half-brother, Don John, relates to family strife and hostility at the top of society.

How might the play have been affected by expectations of Elizabethan theatre?

Elizabethan theatregoers were much more rowdy than modern audiences. Some of Shakespeare's comedy is quite rude in order to appeal to the less-refined members of the audience. For example, Leonato uses a reference to the fake letter in Act 2 scene 3 to joke about Benedick and Beatrice having sex ('she found "Benedick" and "Beatrice" between the sheet'), while Margaret puns on Beatrice's use of the word 'stuffed' (describing her cold) to joke that Beatrice has been sexually penetrated by Benedick ('A maid, and stuffed!').

ven the title is believed to be a rude joke. The word 'thing' was often used as a **euphemism** for the penis; the opposite, 'nothing', would refer to the vagina. There are many romantic situations and problems (much ado) in the play, and desire for women is the root of many of them.

Summary

- The play reflects social conventions with which the Elizabethan audience would have been familiar.
- Comedy is used to subvert some of these conventions before order is restored at the end of the play.
- The title suggests that the play is all about how we judge and gossip about other people, and the consequences of this.
- To appeal to his audience, especially the less-refined theatregoers, Shakespeare includes lots of rude humour.

Questions

QUICK TEST
1. What social conventions are presented in the play?
2. Why is the ending of the play important, in terms of how Shakespeare explored and subverted social conventions during the play?
3. What different interpretations can be made about the play's title?

EXAM PRACTICE
In Act 2 scene 1, Beatrice explains her feelings about men and marriage:
BEATRICE   Just, if He send me no husband; for the which blessing I am at Him upon my knees every morning and evening. Lord, I could not endure a husband with a beard on his face: I had rather lie in the woollen!
LEONATO   You may light on a husband that hath no beard.
BEATRICE   What should I do with him? Dress him in my apparel and make him my waiting-gentlewoman? He that hath a beard is more than a youth, and he that hath no beard is less than a man; and he that is more than a youth is not for me, and he that is less than a man, I am not for him. Therefore, I will even take sixpence in earnest of the bear-ward, and lead his apes into hell.
Write a paragraph explaining how Shakespeare subverts the social conventions of the Elizabethan age.

Comedy and Stagecraft

You must be able to: understand how Shakespeare uses features of genre and stagecraft.

What is a comedy?

When a **Shakespeare** play is classed as a comedy, it usually features humorous language, disguise, romance (and obstacles to it that are overcome) and a happy ending.

Beatrice and Benedick are the main comic characters but humour is also supplied by Dogberry and his men. Comedy is additionally created through Don Pedro's plan to unite Beatrice and Benedick in love. Although Don John tries several schemes to ruin Claudio and Hero's love, the play ends with their marriage and a dance.

Soliloquies

A soliloquy is when a character speaks their thoughts aloud on stage, heard only by the audience. Shakespeare uses soliloquies to reveal romantic feelings and set up comic situations. The important soliloquies in the play come from Benedick in Act 2 scene 3 and Act 5 scene 2, and Beatrice in Act 3 scene 1.

Disguise and concealment

Disguise, mistaken identity and characters hiding in order to observe and listen are key features of Shakespeare's comedies. These techniques often work alongside dramatic irony where the audience knows the truth but one or more characters on stage do not.

The masked party at Leonato's house in Act 2 scene 1 helps to establish a romantic atmosphere for Don Pedro's wooing of Hero on Claudio's behalf. It allows romantic obstacles to be put in place when Don John (pretending that he thinks he is talking to Benedick) lies to Claudio that Don Pedro is in love with Hero. Comedy is also created through Benedick's plan to annoy Beatrice rebounding on him when she describes to the apparent stranger how little she thinks of Benedick.

Concealment is important in Act 2 scene 3 and Act 3 scene 1, where Benedick and Beatrice are tricked into loving each other by their friends. Asides add to the humour by emphasising how the characters are being fooled or allowing the friends to joke about their plan's success.

Disguise and concealment are also used in Don John's plot to make Claudio think Hero is unfaithful, and in the final scene where Claudio discovers that Hero is actually alive.

Wordplay and bawdy humour

Shakespeare includes a lot of **repartee** in the play, where characters quickly respond to each other with witty comments. Often these lines include humorous repetition (a character uses a word from the previous character's speech to continue the conversation), insults, question and answer, wordplay and bawdy humour. Key examples of repartee clude Beatrice and Benedick's conversations in Act 1 scene 1 and Act 2 scene 1, the discussion between Leonato, Antonio and Beatrice at the start of Act 2, and Beatrice, Margaret and Hero's lines in Act 3 scene 4.

Shakespeare also creates humour through the lower-class characters of Dogberry and the Watchmen. They often appear foolish, muddling their words and attempting to speak in a more sophisticated way than they are able. In particular, Dogberry is given lots of **malapropisms**. For example, he tells Borachio and Conrade that their punishment will be 'everlasting redemption' (instead of damnation) in Act 4 scene 2.

Summary

- *Much Ado About Nothing* is a comedy, featuring the key genre elements of humorous language, disguise, romance and a happy ending.
- Shakespeare includes a range of comedy techniques: repartee, repetition, insults, questions and answers, wordplay, bawdiness and malapropisms.
- Soliloquies, asides, disguise, mistaken identity and concealment are used to enhance both the comic and romantic atmospheres.

Questions

QUICK TEST
1. What is a soliloquy?
2. Which two scenes in the play make significant use of concealment to create humour?
3. In what ways does the play have a happy ending?

EXAM PRACTICE
In Act 5 scene 1, Dogberry brings Conrade and Borachio to admit their crimes before Don Pedro and Claudio. Notice Dogberry's confusing speech, and how Don Pedro and Claudio subtly joke about it.

DON PEDRO   Officers, what offence have these men done?

DOGBERRY   Marry, sir, they have committed false report; moreover, they have spoken untruths; secondarily, they are slanders; sixth and lastly, they have belied a lady; thirdly, they have verified unjust things; and, to conclude, they are lying knaves.

DON PEDRO   First, I ask thee what they have done; thirdly, I ask thee what's their offence; sixth and lastly, why they are committed; and, to conclude, what you lay to their charge?

CLAUDIO   Rightly reasoned, and in his own division ...

Write a paragraph explaining how Shakespeare creates comedy in this exchange.

Beatrice

You must be able to: understand how Shakespeare presents Beatrice in the play.

What are the audience's first impressions of Beatrice?

Beatrice is immediately presented as a strong-willed, witty character. She mocks Benedick at the start of Act 1 scene 1, suggesting he will not have fought well in the war: 'But how many hath he killed? For indeed I promised to eat all of his killing'. Shakespeare uses **stichomythia** to emphasise how wittily she undermines all attempts by the Messenger to support Benedick's reputation.

This impression of Beatrice continues when Benedick enters the scene and they mock each other. However, it also suggests how she may be perceived by some men: scornful ('Lady Disdain'), unloving ('so some gentleman or other shall scape a predestinate scratched face') and not worth listening to ('a rare parrot-teacher' means repeating empty words).

Beatrice displays unconventional, cynical attitudes towards men and marriage. In Act 2 scene 1, she claims no man is suitable for her ('he that is more than a youth is not for me; and he that is less than a man I am not for him'). She adds that she would not want to marry and be dominated by someone not her equal: 'Would it not grieve a woman to be over-mastered with a piece of valiant dust?'

Her character is presented as almost equal to the men. In Act 2 scene 1, she speaks frankly – although respectfully – to Don Pedro, despite his status. Furthermore, she displays some control over the proceedings, happily encouraging Claudio and Hero's relationship ('Speak, Count, 'tis your cue … Speak, cousin'). At this point, Don Pedro even proposes to Beatrice. Whether he is serious or not, it highlights that Beatrice's behaviour on stage is meant to always seem good-natured rather than **shrewish**.

How does Shakespeare develop her as a comic figure?

Beatrice is developed as a comic figure through the way in which she is tricked by the other characters. Act 3 scene 2 allows the actor playing Beatrice a lot of physical comedy as she hides to overhear what Hero and Ursula are saying.

This is developed in Act 3 scene 4 when, lovesick for Benedick, Beatrice pretends she merely has a cold. The humour is often focused *on* her, rather than coming *from* her, such as when Margaret jokingly suggests a cure, 'Get you some of this distilled carduus benedictus, and lay it to your heart', in a way that shows she knows the true cause of Beatrice's sickness. It is a humorous contrast to Act 1 where Beatrice appears superior in her wit and self-confidence.

Key Quotations to Learn

(About Benedick) 'In our last conflict, four of his five wits went halting off, and now is the whole man governed with one ...' (Ii)

(To Benedick) 'Is it possible disdain should die, while she hath such meet food to feed it as Signior Benedick?' (Ii)

'I was born to speak all mirth and no matter.' (IIi)

(About Benedick) 'And Benedick, love on, I will requite thee, / Taming my wild heart to thy loving hand.' (IIIi)

Summary

- Beatrice is strong-willed and witty, and appears equal to the male characters.
- She displays unconventional attitudes towards men and marriage.
- She becomes the focus of the jokes when the other characters trick her into love.

Sample Analysis

Beatrice's superiority and unconventional views are presented in her conversation with Leonato in Act 2 scene 1. Her belief that a woman should not 'make an account of her life to a clod of wayward marl' criticises men's dominance in marriage and society. The **nouns** 'clod' and 'marl' compare men to earth, implying that they are low and stupid compared with women, while the **adjective** 'wayward' suggests she sees them as unreliable. It could be argued, however, that Beatrice is merely asserting that a woman should wait for the perfect man rather than be pushed into marriage.

Questions

QUICK TEST
1. How does Beatrice treat Benedick at the start of the play?
2. What appears to be Beatrice's opinion of men?
3. Which important figure proposes to Beatrice and what does this suggest about her?
4. In what way does Beatrice become the target of the characters' jokes?

EXAM PRACTICE
Using one or more of the 'Key Quotations to Learn', write a paragraph analysing how Shakespeare presents Beatrice at the start of the play.

Benedick

You must be able to: understand how Shakespeare presents Benedick in the play.

What are the audience's first impressions of Benedick?

Like Beatrice, Benedick is presented as carefree and witty. He boasts of being popular with women, 'I am loved of all ladies, only you excepted', and makes fun of Beatrice's sharp responses, 'I would my horse had the speed of your tongue'.

His humour appears to be taken in good nature by others. When he jokes that someone else may have fathered Hero, Leonato turns the comment back on him to suggest Benedick is a womaniser: 'no, for then were you a child'.

He doesn't dislike women but, to amuse his friends, presents himself as 'a professed tyrant to their sex'. He uses a **pattern of three**, 'too low for a high praise, too brown for a fair praise, and too little for a great praise', to mock Claudio's attraction, rather than to criticise Hero herself.

Similarly, he humorously over-exaggerates his dismissive attitude to marriage, asking Claudio, 'But I hope you have no intent to turn husband, have you?' before using a **rhetorical question** and **hyperbole**, 'Shall I never see a bachelor of threescore again?', to convey his belief that young men are too eager to get married.

The audience is also shown Benedick's pride through how upset he is when his joke on Beatrice goes wrong at the masked ball. His lines in Act 2 scene 1, 'But that my Lady Beatrice should know me, and not know me! The Prince's fool!', reveal his secret affection for her and how her words have damaged his ego. This is emphasised through a simile when he explains to Don Pedro what happened: 'I stood like a man at a mark, with a whole army shooting at me.'

How does Shakespeare develop him as a comic figure?

Shakespeare **foreshadows** the trick that will be played on Benedick when he says he could only be pale 'with anger, with sickness, or with hunger, my lord, not with love', and is resolute that he will never fall in love and get married.

Again, Beatrice and Benedick mirror each other in that he becomes the target of humour. The use of asides and soliloquy in Act 2 scene 3 highlight the way in which Benedick is fooled into admitting to himself his love for Beatrice: 'When I said I would die a bachelor, I did not think I should live till I were married.'

This is further emphasised when he looks for double meaning in Beatrice's words as evidence that she loves him and when he tries to hide his lovesickness from Don Pedro and Claudio by claiming he has toothache (just as Beatrice claims to have a cold), only for them to continually joke about how they 'conclude he is in love'.

Key Quotations to Learn

(To Beatrice) 'What, my dear Lady Disdain! Are you yet living?' (Ii)

...oking what his friends should do if he falls in love) '... pick out mine eyes with a ballad-maker's pen, and hang me at the door of a brothel house for the sign of blind Cupid.' (Ii)

(About Beatrice's words) 'Oh she misused me past the endurance of a block!' (IIi)

...ove me? Why it must be requited ... I have railed so long against marriage, but doth ...ot the appetite alter?' (IIiii)

Summary

Benedick is carefree and witty, often making humorous criticisms of love and marriage.

He has a lot of pride and this is hurt when Beatrice mocks him at the masked ball.

He becomes a target of Don Pedro's and Claudio's jokes.

He and Beatrice mirror each other in terms of their behaviour, how the other characters trick them, and how they try to hide their lovesickness from their friends.

Sample Analysis

Benedick's pride is shown at the masked ball in Act 2 scene 1 after his trick on Beatrice rebounds on him. The **metaphor** 'she speaks poniards, and every word stabs' conveys how he has been hurt by Beatrice's opinions. The dagger imagery links to his role as a soldier and how his position alongside Don Pedro has given him social status; the way Beatrice has mocked this position has damaged his ego. His apparent unhappiness that she finds him dull and foolish also reveals his secret affection for her: he cares about her opinions of him.

Questions

QUICK TEST

. What is Benedick's attitude towards marriage?
. Why does Benedick act so dismissively of women?
3. How does Beatrice upset Benedick?
. In what ways do Benedick and Beatrice mirror each other?

EXAM PRACTICE

Using one or more of the 'Key Quotations to Learn', write a paragraph analysing how Shakespeare presents Benedick at the start of the play.

Beatrice and Benedick's Development

You must be able to: understand how Shakespeare develops Beatrice and Benedick in the play.

How is love between Beatrice and Benedick presented?

After the comic portrayal of their love, the crisis in Act 4 brings Beatrice and Benedick together. When the soldiers leave the wedding, Benedick stays. He tries to lessen Leonato's anger towards Hero, 'Sir, sir, be patient', and seeks evidence of Hero's innocence through Beatrice: 'Lady, were you her bedfellow last night?' Matching the serious situation, and reflecting the realisation of their feelings, their speech is now mature and serious.

Initially too proud to fully speak their feelings, they share an awkward admission of their love that is also phrased to hide it. Benedick's words, 'I do love nothing in the world so well as you', could mean he values her highly or he doesn't value her at all. Her response, 'I loved nothing so well as you', has the same dual meaning.

Eventually, matching each other's language to emphasise their bond, they pronounce their love: 'I protest I love thee' and 'I was about to protest I loved you.'

How is a serious side to Beatrice and Benedick presented?

Beatrice's struggle with her feelings suggests a vulnerable side to her character. This is hinted at in Act 2 scene 1 when she refers to a past relationship with Benedick, 'he lent it me awhile, and I gave him use for it, a double heart for his single one … he won it of me with false dice', implying that she gave more love than was returned and that he was possibly unfaithful (the adjective 'false').

Beatrice is loyal and determined. She stands by Hero, 'O, on my soul, my cousin is belied!', emphasising this through her pattern of three, 'She is wronged, she is slandered, she is undone', and her demand that Benedick 'Kill Claudio!' When he falters, she shows her anger at men's unreliability and society's gender inequalities: 'O God, that I were a man! I would eat his heart in the market-place.' When Benedick agrees to Beatrice's demand, he challenges Claudio, accuses him and Don Pedro of having 'killed a sweet and innocent lady' and gives up his position in the army. Despite initial disbelief and mockery from Don Pedro and Claudio, Benedick acts with dignity and honour.

How do Beatrice and Benedick end the play?

Upon realising they have been tricked by their friends, Shakespeare's use of repetition highlights both the comedy and how well-matched they are: 'They swore that you were almost sick for me'; 'They swore that you were well-nigh dead for me.'

Instead of a romantic declaration, they joke with each other before kissing. Benedick says he will take her out of 'pity' and Beatrice says she will 'yield upon great persuasion'.

The change in Benedick's character is highlighted by his final words to Don Pedro: 'Get thee a wife, get thee a wife!'

Key Quotations to Learn

Benedick:	'By this hand, I love thee.' / Beatrice: 'Use it for my love some other way than swearing by it.' (IVi)
Benedick:	'I do suffer love indeed, for I love thee against my will.' / Beatrice: 'In spite of your heart, I think.' (Vii)
Benedick:	'Thou and I are too wise to woo peaceably.' (Vii)

Summary

- Benedick and Beatrice find it hard to admit their love for one another.
- The later scenes of the play show Beatrice's vulnerability, loyalty and determination.
- The serious, dignified and honourable aspects of Benedick's character are revealed.
- Their love is sealed with joking and a kiss.

Sample Analysis

Beatrice and Benedick's continual denial of their love is used by Shakespeare for comic effect. In the final scene, Benedick's question, 'Do not you love me?', receives the reply, 'Why, no, no more than reason.' Beatrice's dispassionate response contrasts humorously with his emotional request. Their amusing stubbornness is also highlighted through the way she only gives half a denial, emphasised by the pause created through the repetition of 'no'; at the same time, his words focus on her love for him rather than actually admitting his own feelings. However, Shakespeare arranges their words so they share the same line of verse, indicating that they are well-matched and can't escape their love.

Questions

QUICK TEST
1. What event helps to bring Beatrice and Benedick together?
2. What does Beatrice ask Benedick to do and how does he respond?
3. How does their love continue to be unconventional at the end of the play?

EXAM PRACTICE
Using one or more of the 'Key Quotations to Learn', write a paragraph analysing how Shakespeare presents Beatrice and Benedick's relationship in the later scenes of the play.

Characters > Hero

You must be able to: understand how Shakespeare presents Hero in the play.

How is Hero presented in Act 1?

Unlike Beatrice, Hero barely speaks in her first scene. Instead, she is presented through Claudio's perception of her. His attraction is linked to conventional expectations of women: her silence and virtue ('modest young lady') and her beauty (his 'jewel' metaphor). He uses the superlative adjective 'sweetest' to suggest these qualities stand out. The importance of her beauty and innocence is indicated by the men's repeated use of the adjective 'fair' when describing her.

Typically, Hero is presented as an object. Benedick alludes to this when he asks Claudio, 'Would you buy her, that you inquire after her?' It can also be seen in Don Pedro's words when he assures Claudio that 'she shall be thine' and later describes her as 'won'.

How does Shakespeare develop her character?

At the start of Act 2, Hero displays the quality of obedience. When asked if she will be 'ruled' by Leonato's wishes, her lack of reply suggests that her obedience was never in question. Beatrice appears to mock her cousin's sense of 'duty' whilst accepting its normality.

She responds to Don Pedro's wooing with politeness and restraint, once more remaining silent when her forthcoming marriage to Claudio is announced.

Hero's acceptance of how she should behave in front of men is highlighted by how contrastingly talkative she is in the company of women at the start of Act 3. The scene shows that she can be perceptive, confident, witty and mischievous. She guesses how Beatrice will fall for their trick, gives orders to Margaret and Ursula, uses the 'lapwing' simile to mock how Beatrice eavesdrops on their conversation, and appears to have fun using lists and hyperbole to describe Benedick's qualities and how much he is in love.

She makes some defence when confronted by Claudio on her wedding day: 'O God defend me, how am I beset!' However, her role as a weak victim is emphasised by how she '[swoons]' and hardly speaks again until the final scene where she again shows her virtue by forgiving Claudio and emphasising her virginity: 'And surely as I live, I am a maid.'

Key Quotations to Learn

Claudio: 'Can the world buy such a jewel?' (Ii)

Beatrice: '... it is my cousin's duty to make curtsy and say, "Father, as it please you."' (IIi)

Hero: '[Aside] ... Some Cupid kills with arrows, some with traps.' (IIIi)

Hero: 'If I know more of any man alive / Than that which maiden modesty doth
            warrant, / Let all my sins lack mercy!' (IVi)

Summary

- Hero is presented as an ideal wife: she is virtuous, quiet, obedient and beautiful.
- She does not have many lines so her character is often presented through the eyes of others (particularly Claudio).
- Her reserved behaviour contrasts with that of Beatrice.
- Hero is much more confident, witty and fun when in the company of women.

Sample Analysis

Shakespeare creates sympathy for Hero through her desperation for her father to believe in her innocence. She uses a pattern of three, 'Refuse me, hate me, torture me to death!', to emphasise her lack of guilt by saying what Leonato can do should Claudio's accusation be proven. Linking to the importance of a woman's virtuous reputation, the increasing intensity of the **verb phrases** indicates her anguish and horror at how she is doubted by her own father. The final reference to death highlights how her life will be metaphorically over if the slander against her is believed.

Questions

QUICK TEST
1. What qualities is Hero praised for at the start of the play?
2. What is unusual about how Hero's character is conveyed in the play?
3. How does she appear to change when in the company of women rather than men?
4. What virtues of Hero's are emphasised in the final scene?

EXAM PRACTICE
Using one or more of the 'Key Quotations to Learn', write a paragraph analysing how Shakespeare presents Hero in the play.

Claudio

You must be able to: understand how Shakespeare presents Claudio in the play.

How is Claudio presented as a conventional character?

Like Hero, Claudio provides a conventional image of romance. He falls quickly in love, based on appearance, 'how fair young Hero is', and the feminine ideal of the time: 'Is she not a modest young lady?'

He is honest about his feelings and how he is changed by love, using **personification** to describe how it has replaced his previous focus on the war: 'in their rooms / Come thronging soft and delicate desires'. This change in attitude allows Shakespeare to create humour, using repetition, dramatic pauses, a rhetorical question and gentle insults to portray Benedick's shock at Claudio's transformation: 'on my allegiance, mark you this, on my allegiance – he is in love. With who? ... Leonato's short daughter.'

Shakespeare later shows Claudio's comedic side when he has fun tricking (such as the hunting metaphor, '[*Aside to Don Pedro*] Stalk on, stalk on, the fowl sits') and mocking Benedick.

In what ways is Claudio honourable?

Claudio is first described through the honour that he has won in the war despite his youth: 'doing, in the figure of a lamb, the feats of a lion.'

He courts Hero honourably, with Don Pedro acting as a go-between to broach the subject with Hero and, importantly, her father (showing respect for tradition). He worries that his sudden love could appear improper, 'lest my liking might too sudden seem', and shows his devotion, 'I give away myself for you'.

Later, Claudio accepts the wrong he has done Hero. The metaphor 'I have drunk poison whiles he utter'd it' conveys his guilt upon hearing Borachio's explanation. He tells Leonato to 'Choose your revenge', and compares his behaviour to **sin**: 'Impose me to what penance your invention / Can lay upon my sin.' He instantly accepts Leonato's punishments and pledges to repeat Hero's epitaph annually: 'Yearly will I do this rite.'

What are the negative aspects of Claudio's character?

Claudio's sudden love can be seen as immature. The audience see him 'shake the head' with impatience when Leonato decides he must wait until Monday to get married.

He is easily fooled and shows a distrust of women. Don John tricks him into believing that Don Pedro is wooing Hero for himself, causing him to sulk ('I wish him joy of her'), and then convinces him she has been disloyal.

His wish to publicly 'shame' Hero at the wedding is cruel. He calls her a 'rotten orange' and says, 'She's but the sign and semblance of her honour', suggesting her beauty and modesty hide sin. However, the belief he has been betrayed causes him unhappiness: the metaphor 'For thee I'll lock up all the gates of love' could refer to Hero or how he now feels about all women

Key Quotations to Learn

'In mine eye, she is the sweetest lady that ever I looked on.' (Ii)

'Time goes on crutches till love have all his rites.' (IIi)

'I never tempted her with word too large, / But, as a brother to his sister, show'd / Bashful sincerity and comely love.' (IVi)

(To Hero) 'But fare thee well, most foul, most fair! Farewell, / Thou pure impiety and impious purity.' (IVi)

Summary

- In comparison with Benedick, Claudio is a more conventional romantic character.
- He is honourable in his wooing of Hero and hurt by her apparent betrayal.
- It can be argued that Claudio is immature, rash and too easily influenced.
- He is also given a comic side through his enjoyment of tricking Benedick.

Sample Analysis

Claudio is presented as angry and disgusted when his romantic idealism of Hero is apparently disproven. The simile 'Behold how like a maid she blushes here!' in Act 4 scene 1 shows him questioning her virginity and suggesting that she masks her true self. Unlike men, unmarried women at the time were expected to be sexually innocent. His public denouncement of Hero, emphasised by the word 'behold', may seem cruel but it is based on his disillusionment. When he adds 'cunning sin cover itself', the adjective and verb continue to focus on the idea that he has been deceived while the use of religious language highlights what he sees as the extremity of Hero's immorality.

Questions

QUICK TEST
1. What does Claudio's attraction to Hero appear to be based on?
2. In what way does Claudio display impatience about love?
3. What two instances suggest that Claudio is easily tricked?
4. How does he behave honourably towards the end of the play?

EXAM PRACTICE
Using one or more of the 'Key Quotations to Learn', write a paragraph analysing how Shakespeare presents Claudio in the play.

Don Pedro

You must be able to: understand how Shakespeare presents Don Pedro in the play.

How is Don Pedro presented as having status and honour?

Don Pedro is the Prince of Aragon. Leonato speaks to him respectfully ('your Grace') and, despite his higher status, Don Pedro returns that respect. This status is also shown through the implication that Leonato agrees to take in the army for a month at his own expense.

Despite his friendliness with his men, they address him respectfully (Claudio: 'My liege, your Highness') and he is shown giving orders (such as to Benedick). He also uses the verb 'teach' several times, suggesting that he is valued for his life experience.

The simile 'Runs not this speech like iron through your blood?' conveys his shock when he hears Borachio's confession. He displays guilt for having acted dishonourably and says he will do anything, 'bend under any heavy weight', to earn Leonato's forgiveness.

How is Don Pedro linked to comedy and romance?

Don Pedro approves of Claudio's attraction to Hero, takes control of the courtship and is confident of its success: 'thou lovest, / And I will fit thee with the remedy.' When he woos her, some of his lines are written as a quatrain of poetry to emphasise his romantic skills. However, he is single and his proposal to Beatrice appears only half in jest.

He also devises the plan to bring Benedick and Beatrice together. He makes jokes at Benedick's expense during the orchard scene (Claudio: 'And she is exceeding wise.' / Don Pedro: 'In everything but in loving Benedick.') and when Benedick pretends his lovesickness is toothache (Claudio: '… I know who loves him.' / Don Pedro: '… I warrant, one that knows him not.').

What negative characteristics does Don Pedro display?

His pride is shown in the way he sees Hero's apparent betrayal of Claudio as a personal slight: 'I stand dishonour'd, that have gone about / To link my dear friend to a common stale.' He is fooled by his brother and, typical for the time in which the play is set, too ready to believe a man over a woman.

Although he claims to feel sympathy, 'My heart is sorry for your daughter's death', he appears callous when he speaks to Leonato: 'But, on my honour, she was charg'd with nothing / But what was true, and very full of proof' (with the **enjambment** cleverly alluding to his mistake). This is emphasised by how he and Claudio then joke about Leonato and Antonio's anger: 'What think'st thou? Had we fought, I doubt we should have been too young for them.'

Key Quotations to Learn

Leonato: 'Please it your Grace to lead on?' / Don Pedro: 'Your hand, Leonato, we will go together.' (Ii)

'Amen, if you love her, for the lady is very well worthy.' (Ii)

(On tricking Benedick and Beatrice) '[Aside] Let there be the same net spread for her ... the sport will be when they hold one an opinion of another's dotage ...' (IIiii)

Summary

As Prince of Aragon, Don Pedro is highly respected.

He shows respect to others and has a friendly relationship with his men, despite remaining their superior.

Shakespeare creates comedy through Don Pedro's mockery of Benedick.

He displays a romantic side but joins Claudio in the shaming of Hero, coming to regret his dishonourable behaviour when the truth is revealed.

Sample Analysis

Following social expectations of the time, Don Pedro values his men over women. When he says to Claudio 'And as I wooed for thee to obtain her, I will join with thee to disgrace her', the repetition of 'I' and 'thee' suggests a comradeship that is highlighted by Shakespeare's use of parallelism. The verb 'obtain' suggests that, despite his romantic nature, Don Pedro still sees women as objects to win. The cruel plan to publicly 'disgrace' Hero indicates how quick he is to judge a woman while also linking to his wish to protect Claudio's – and his own – sense of honour.

Questions

QUICK TEST

. How is Don Pedro's status reflected in the way people speak to him?
. How does Don Pedro react to Claudio's attraction to Hero?
. Who does Don Pedro often make jokes about?
. How is Don Pedro's condemnation of Hero linked to his sense of personal pride?

EXAM PRACTICE

Using one or more of the 'Key Quotations to Learn', write a paragraph analysing how Shakespeare presents Don Pedro in the play.

You must be able to: understand how Shakespeare presents Leonato in the play.

How is Leonato presented in Act 1 scene 1?

Leonato values life and happiness. Talking of the war, he says, 'A victory is twice itself when the achiever brings home full numbers', before showing good will towards Claudio's uncle who will be 'very much glad' of his son's elevated status. He praises **benevolence**, saying of people who cry tears of kindness, 'There are no faces truer than those that are so washed.' He generously invites the army to stay for a month.

His outlook on life possibly makes Leonato **naive**. The problems ahead are foreshadowed when he tells Don Pedro 'Never came trouble to my house in the likeness of your Grace'.

How does Leonato respond to Benedick and Beatrice?

Leonato finds Beatrice and Benedick's relationship amusing, using the military metaphors a 'merry war' and a 'skirmish of wit'. He shows mock sympathy towards Benedick ('you tax Signior Benedick too much') whilst saying he is a match for her ('but he'll be meet with you').

Although Leonato would like Beatrice to be 'one day fitted with a husband', he accepts her attitude towards men and jokes with her. However, his attitude towards his own daughter is more patriarchal, reminding her that 'you know your answer' when they think Don Pedro may ask to marry her.

He shows quick-wittedness when he jokes with Benedick after the latter makes a bawdy comment that **implies** someone else might be Hero's father. He is also happy to join in Don Pedro's plan to unite Beatrice and Benedick.

To what extent is Leonato presented as honourable?

Leonato is proud to see Hero marrying Claudio. When he misunderstands Claudio's accusation and thinks he is admitting to having slept with her already ('made defeat of her virginity'), Leonato is willing to forgive Claudio.

When the accusation is made clear, Leonato sees it as a loss of personal honour: 'Hath no man's dagger here a point for me?' His subsequent behaviour would have seemed natural in the 16th century but, for a modern audience, appears dishonourable. Because of his patriarchal values, he trusts men of status more than his daughter and wishes her dead: 'Would the two princes lie, would Claudio lie? … Hence from her. Let her die!'

Reflecting Sicily's Catholicism, he refers to Hero's 'damnation'. He often seems selfish rather than loving, 'My griefs cry louder than advertisement', but gradually realises – in his 'soul' – that his daughter is innocent. As a mark of honour, he challenges Claudio to a duel for having 'belied my innocent child; / Thy slander hath gone through and through her heart'.

When the truth is revealed, he uses **irony** to denounce Don Pedro's and Claudio's lack of honour: 'Record it with your high and worthy deeds; / 'Twas bravely done …' However, he accepts their remorse and forgives them.

Key Quotations to Learn

'Count, take of me my daughter, and with her my fortunes; his Grace hath made the match, and all grace say "Amen" to it.' (IIi)

'Death is the fairest cover for her shame / That may be wished for.' (IVi)

(Challenging Claudio to a duel) 'I'll prove it on his body if he dare, / Despite his nice fence and his active practice, / His May of youth and bloom of lustihood.' (Vi)

Summary

- Leonato is a cheerful and generous man who shows good will to others. He accepts Beatrice's attitude towards men but has more patriarchal expectations of Hero.

- Leonato initially believes the accusations against his daughter. Taking them as a mark against his own honour, he wishes her dead.

- Beginning to believe in Hero's innocence, he challenges Claudio to a duel. When the truth is revealed, he forgives Claudio and Don Pedro.

Sample Analysis

Shakespeare uses Leonato's sense of honour and patriarchal values to portray the father's conflicting attitudes towards his shamed daughter. When he says, 'If they speak but truth of her, / These hands shall tear her', his anger towards Hero for the shame she has brought him is conveyed by the aggressive verb 'tear'. However, his subsequent lines, 'If they wrong her honour, / The proudest of them shall well hear of it', display his readiness to defend his daughter's (and, by extension, his own) reputation. The superlative adjective 'proudest' refers to the acclaim Claudio has won in the war but also links to Leonato's own sense of pride.

Questions

QUICK TEST

1. How are Leonato's attitudes towards Beatrice and Hero portrayed differently?
2. In what ways is Leonato honourable?
3. Why might a modern audience consider Leonato to be dishonourable?

EXAM PRACTICE

Using one or more of the 'Key Quotations to Learn', write a paragraph analysing how Shakespeare presents Leonato in the play.

Don John, Borachio and Conrade

You must be able to: understand how Shakespeare presents Don John and his allies in the play

How does Don John form a contrast to the other characters?

Don John is the villain of the play. Whilst Messina seems a happy place, Don John is miserable. He calls his sadness 'without limit' and says he can 'smile at no man's jests'. Beatrice jokes how she feels 'heart-burned' by how sharply he looks at others.

The play's comedy regularly focuses on uniting lovers. Don John wishes to create discord, hoping to see 'the death of this marriage' and repeatedly using the word 'cross' to describe his plans to put obstacles between Claudio and Hero.

Secrecy and masks are often used to create romance and comedy but they also show Don John's dishonesty. He uses the masked ball to trick Claudio then presents himself as a respectful and moral man: 'My lord and brother, God save you! … Means your lordship to be married tomorrow?'

Many characters display their honour but Don John admits he 'cannot be said to be a flattering honest man' and, instead, calls himself 'a plain-dealing villain'. The contrasting adjectives imply that he thinks nice people are actually false. Later, rather than accept his guilt, he flees.

What is Don John's motivation?

Don John is looked down on due to his illegitimacy, 'your brother the Bastard', and there has been a disagreement – now forgiven – between him and Don Pedro: 'You have of late stood out against your brother'. He sees himself as an outcast, 'I had rather be a canker in a hedge than a rose in his grace'. This appears to have shaped his behaviour, 'it better fits my blood to be disdained of all than to fashion a carriage to rob love from any', suggesting that he'd rather be hated than try to get people to like him.

He dislikes Claudio because he feels he should be the man closest to Don Pedro: 'That young start-up hath all the glory of my overthrow.' He criticises Claudio's youth, 'A very forward March-chick!', and suggests he is presumptuous for falling in love with Hero. Claudio's happiness causes him unhappiness: 'I am sick in displeasure to him'.

How does Shakespeare present Borachio and Conrade?

Conrade tries to raise Don John's spirits: 'why are you thus out of measure sad?' Using the metaphor 'frame the season for your own harvest', he advises him to improve his status by manipulating Don Pedro's good will. He promises that Don John can rely on him 'to the death'.

Borachio is even more of a troublemaker. He finds out others' secrets ('I whipped me behind the arras, and there heard it') and proudly forms the plan to slander Hero: 'my cunning shall not shame me.' Borachio's boastful pride in his villainy, 'I have earned of Don John a thousand ducats', leads to his capture. To his credit, he feels guilt at the end of the play and insists Margaret was innocent of the plan.

Key Quotations to Learn

'… I have decreed not to sing in my cage.' (Iiii)

(Referring to Claudio) 'If I can cross him any way, I bless myself every way.' (Iiii)

(Referring to Claudio and Hero's marriage) 'Any bar, any cross, any impediment will be medicinable to me.' (IIi)

(Slandering Hero) Claudio: 'Disloyal?' / Don John: 'The word is too good to paint out her wickedness.' (IIIii)

Summary

- Don John is a villain and resents Claudio's closeness with Don Pedro.
- He feels looked down on due to his illegitimacy, and this appears to have shaped his behaviour.
- He is miserable and seeks others' unhappiness; he is dishonourable and dishonest.
- Conrade and Borachio are his allies. Borachio, in particular, is proud of his villainy.

Sample Analysis

Shakespeare presents Don John and Borachio as scheming villains. When Borachio describes his plan to 'misuse the Prince, to vex Claudio, to undo Hero, and kill Leonato', the increasingly cruel verbs convey his malignity and this is emphasised by how the list builds up his number of innocent victims. Don John's response, 'to despite them I will endeavour anything', shows that he dedicates his life to the misery of others and implies that this is his only source of happiness. Although the play links his behaviour to his illegitimacy, and the disrespect that this would have brought in the 16th century, the verb 'despite' indicates that his actions are based on an irrational desire to hurt others rather than gain revenge.

Questions

QUICK TEST

1. How does Don John contrast with the happy atmosphere of Messina?
2. What does Don John appear to resent about Claudio?
3. What does Don John do when his plot against Claudio is revealed?
4. Who forms the plan to slander Hero?

EXAM PRACTICE

Using one or more of the 'Key Quotations to Learn', write a paragraph analysing how Shakespeare presents Don John in the play.

Dogberry and Margaret

You must be able to: understand how Shakespeare presents Dogberry and Margaret in the play.

How is Dogberry presented?

Dogberry is the master constable. He is a proud man and takes his position seriously; Shakespeare makes him a comic figure by juxtaposing this with his lack of intelligence and the muddled way in which he undertakes his duties (such as the interrogation in Act 4 scene 2).

Comedy is created through Dogberry's malapropisms, for example inadvertently criticising the second watchman as 'desartless' and 'senseless' when he means 'deserving' and 'sensible'. This is heightened when he speaks to Leonato and tries to raise the sophistication of his speech to appear impressive (such as using 'aspicious', or auspicious, instead of 'suspicious').

Although they are unfamiliar to a modern audience, Dogberry uses lots of proverbs. This suggests that he wants to seem wise, particularly in front of Leonato: 'As they say, "When the age is in, the wit is out."' Partly because of all the proverbs, his speech is rambling and repetitive. The humour of this is emphasised when placed in a situation where there isn't much time (such as Act 3 scene 4 when Leonato is preparing for the wedding ceremony).

Dogberry's incompetence is highlighted in Act 5 scene 1 where he cannot present the evidence in a proper order: 'secondarily … sixth and lastly … thirdly'. His foolishness is mirrored by that of his companions, Verges and the watchmen, but it is important to remember that while they are comic figures who are mocked by the other characters (Leonato calls them 'tedious' and Don Pedro sarcastically calls Dogberry 'learned'), they are also, in Leonato's words, 'honest'.

How is Margaret presented?

Margaret is Hero's lady-in-waiting. She is given some quite long speeches to show that she is talkative (for example, about Hero's wedding dress or on the topic of bawdy humour) and Beatrice comments on the 'pace' of her tongue.

She shocks Hero when she jokes about sex. She uses comic double meanings, such as linking Beatrice's cold to sexual intercourse ('A maid, and stuffed!') and hinting that Beatrice is lovesick for Benedick by referring to a medicinal herb called 'carduus benedictus'.

She has fun aggravating Beatrice. Using parallelism for comic effect, she innocently pretends that she would never suggest Beatrice is in love ('I cannot think … that you are in love, or that you will be in love, or that you can be in love'). However, she then adds that Beatrice probably is in love ('but methinks you look with your eyes as other women do').

She is called 'good' and 'sweet' by other characters. When Leonato suspects she was part of the plot against Hero, Borachio insists she was innocent, 'just and virtuous'.

Key Quotations to Learn

Dogberry: '... for the watch to babble and to talk is most tolerable, and not to be endured.' (IIIiii)

Dogberry: 'But masters, remember that I am an ass: though it be not written down, yet forget not that I am an ass.' (IVii)

Margaret: ''Twill be heavier soon by the weight of a man.' / Hero: 'Fie upon thee, art not ashamed?' (IIIiv)

Summary

- Dogberry and Margaret are comic figures with lower social status.
- Dogberry is characterised by his malapropisms and general incompetence which contrast with his wish to appear intelligent and in control.
- Margaret is very talkative, makes rude jokes and enjoys annoying Beatrice. She is duped into becoming part of the plot against Hero.
- Despite their faults, both characters are praised at different points for their goodness.

Sample Analysis

Shakespeare creates comedy through Dogberry's speech. His characteristic malapropisms can be seen in Act 3 scene 4, 'One word, sir: our watch, sir, have indeed comprehended two aspicious persons', where he uses the wrong word for apprehended and also sounds like he is praising the criminals. His attempts to heighten his language in front of Leonato could be interpreted as hubris or respect. Dogberry's repetition of 'sir' displays his wish to appear formal and professional but it is undermined by how his promise of 'one word' contrasts with his rambling speech. This is later emphasised by his mispronunciation of sufficient as 'suffigance'.

Questions

QUICK TEST
1. What do Dogberry and Margaret have in common?
2. Why does Dogberry try to heighten the complexity of his language?
3. Why is Dogberry contrastingly mocked and praised?
4. Who does Margaret enjoy annoying?

EXAM PRACTICE
Using one or more of the 'Key Quotations to Learn', write a paragraph analysing how Shakespeare presents Dogberry in the play.

Gender

You must be able to: understand how Shakespeare presents the theme of gender in the play.

How does Shakespeare present gender expectations?

Sixteenth-century expectations of the ideal woman are presented through Hero: she is attractive, modest and submissive. Shakespeare conveys this through how other characters speak about her (such as Don Pedro repeating the adjective 'fair') and the way she behaves (for example, silently obeying her father's wishes). She is also weak and requires saving by others, shown by how she faints at the wedding and needs the help of Benedick and the Friar.

In comparison, men are linked to honour and strength: the Messenger refers to Benedick's 'honourable virtues' and how Claudio has 'bettered expectation'; many of the central male characters are soldiers and duelling is mentioned several times.

Women are mistrusted and seen as inferior to men. Claudio is quick to doubt Hero; thinking Don Pedro has wooed her for himself, Claudio uses personification to blame Hero's looks, 'beauty is a witch / Against whose charms faith melteth into blood.' He also later refers to Hero's 'mischief' when Don John makes his false claims.

How are ideas about gender subverted?

Beatrice is used to present a less conventional view of women. Although also described as 'fair', she is characterised by her 'wit'. She openly mocks men ('a piece of valiant dust'), disdains marriage ('if He send me no husband, for the which blessing I am at Him'), and criticises patriarchal values ('make another curtsy and say, "Father, as it please you"').

Beatrice is also perceptive and guesses that Claudio thinks Don Pedro has wooed Hero for himself. Making a pun on Seville oranges and their almost yellow rind (the colour **traditionally** linked to jealousy), she describes Claudio as a 'civil Count, civil as an orange, and something of that jealous complexion'.

The men are often presented as lacking judgement. Claudio and Don Pedro are easily fooled – even though Don John has only recently been reconciled with his brother, they trust him more than Hero, partly because he is a man and partly because personal honour is so important. Seeing this immaturity, Antonio calls them 'Boys, apes, braggarts, jacks, milksops!'

How does Shakespeare explore the battle of the sexes?

Beatrice and Benedick are used to humorously examine the differences between men and women, and how expectations of gender cause conflict. Leonato describes their antagonism as a 'merry war' and 'skirmish of wit'.

Benedick believes he cannot 'trust' women and makes many jokes related to 'horns' (the traditional symbol for a man whose wife has cheated on him). Saying she wouldn't want a husband until 'God make men of some other metal than earth', Beatrice suggests that men have too many flaws that mean they aren't good enough for women.

imately, however, the way in which they are both fooled and continue to deny their
utual love through matching language indicates that men and women have more
ilarities than they may initially think.

Key Quotations to Learn

Antonio: 'Well, niece, I trust you will be ruled by your father.' (IIi)

Don Pedro: '... fair Hero is won ... In faith, lady, you have a merry heart.' (IIi)

Benedick: 'They swore that you were almost sick for me.' / Beatrice: 'They swore that
            you were well-nigh dead for me.' (Viv)

Summary

Characters such as Claudio and Hero present traditional gender expectations.

These expectations are subverted through Beatrice's intelligence and sense of
humour, and the way in which Claudio and Don Pedro make big errors of judgement.

Beatrice and Benedick are used to explore gender conflict and the idea that men
and women are different. However, Shakespeare shows us that they are similar and
suggests love is stronger than conflict.

Sample Analysis

Traditional gender roles are explored through Claudio's attraction to Hero. When he
says, 'In mine eye, she is the sweetest lady that ere I looked on', the combination of the
noun 'eye' and the verb 'looked' suggest that she is valued for her beauty rather than
her mind. This repetition of imagery linked to the male gaze also indicates the power
of men in the 16th century and their control over courtship, aspects of the play that a
modern audience might question. Claudio's use of the superlative adjective 'sweetest'
also links to traditional expectations of the ideal women as it is Hero's silence, modesty
and implied inferiority that make her attractive to her future husband.

Questions

QUICK TEST

1.   How is Hero's behaviour linked to traditional ideals of female behaviour?
2.   What traditional signs of masculinity do Claudio, Benedick and Don Pedro display?
3.   Does Beatrice conform to or subvert traditional expectations of gender?
4.   In what way does Benedick not trust women?

EXAM PRACTICE

Using one or more of the 'Key Quotations to Learn', write a paragraph analysing how
Shakespeare presents the theme of gender in the play.

Love and Courtship

You must be able to: understand how Shakespeare presents the themes of love and courtship in the play.

How does Shakespeare present love in a traditional way?

Just as Claudio and Hero are used to represent traditional gender roles, Shakespeare uses the couple to create a traditional depiction of love. Whilst it is not quite love at first sight for Claudio (he previously 'look'd upon her with a soldier's eye'), he experiences a sudden realisation of emotions that is described through personification: 'Come thronging soft and delicate desires, / All prompting me how fair young Hero is …'

Traditionally, being in love was often linked to unhappiness, pain or sickness until the emotion was **requited**. Claudio refers to 'love's grief' and Don Pedro tells him 'thou lovest, / And I will fit thee with the remedy'.

Love is often represented through images of unity and, once their marriage is decided, Shakespeare uses parallelism to convey Claudio's commitment: 'Lady, as you are mine, I am yours.'

How are traditional images of courtship used?

In the 16th century, it was expected that a man would try to win his lover's heart. The idea of a woman as a prize to be fought for and attained can be seen when Claudio refers to Hero a 'a jewel' and Don Pedro announces that 'fair Hero is won'. Additionally, the language of war is included in Don Pedro's metaphor 'I'll unclasp my heart, / And take her hearing prisoner'.

It was also common for a woman to test a man's love, such as when Beatrice challenges Benedick to kill Claudio on her behalf.

Parental permission and etiquette were also important aspects of courtship. While Don Pedro encourages Claudio, saying he 'wilt be like a lover presently' and telling him to 'cherish' his feelings, he highlights the importance of broaching the matter ('break') with Leonato. Claudio is keen for his courtship to appear respectable and worries that his 'liking might too sudden seem'.

How is Benedick and Beatrice's love more unconventional?

Beatrice and Benedick spend most of the play arguing and are ultimately tricked into love. However, it could be argued that their love is truer as they are more evenly matched and their emotions based more on personality than looks.

Shakespeare uses their love to explore the idea that people's attitudes to one another change, 'doth not the appetite alter?', and that love makes one a better person: 'happy are they that hear their detractions and can put them to mending.'

Shakespeare also explores the notion that people can be too 'proud' to admit their emotions. This is used to create humour in the scenes where Benedick and Beatrice pretend that the pain traditionally associated with love is a genuine illness (his toothache and her cold).

Key Quotations to Learn

Claudio: 'That I love her, I feel.' / Don Pedro: 'That she is worthy, I know.' (Ii)

Benedick: 'Love me? Why, it must be requited!' (IIiii)

Hero: 'My talk to thee must be how Benedick / Is sick in love with Beatrice. Of this matter / Is little Cupid's crafty arrow made ...' (IIIi)

Beatrice: 'Contempt, farewell, and maiden pride, adieu!' (IIIi)

Summary

- Claudio and Hero present a more traditional image of love.
- Love is traditionally associated with unhappiness, pain and illness until it is requited.
- It is the man's role to respectfully court a woman and gain her love, although her father's agreement is also important.
- Benedick and Beatrice's love is more unconventional but arguably truer.

Sample Analysis

Traditional images of the pain of unrequited love are exaggerated for comic effect in Act 2 scene 3. Claudio falsely claims that Beatrice '... falls, weeps, sobs, beats her heart, tears her hair, prays, curses: "O sweet Benedick ...!"' in order to present her love as genuine. The list of increasingly powerful verbs builds up an image of love that is simultaneously conventional and ridiculous. The dramatic irony of the audience knowing Benedick is being tricked makes the language humorous for us while it seems realistic for him. The final exclamation, with its use of the amorous adjective 'sweet', adds to the humour as it is manipulating Benedick's characteristic pride.

Questions

QUICK TEST
1. How is love traditionally linked to more negative feelings?
2. What is courtship?
3. How does Beatrice want Benedick to prove his love for her?
4. What emotion stops Benedick and Beatrice admitting their feelings?

EXAM PRACTICE
Using one or more of the 'Key Quotations to Learn', write a paragraph analysing how Shakespeare presents the theme of love in the play.

Marriage and Infidelity

You must be able to: understand how Shakespeare presents the themes of marriage and infidelity in the play.

How does the play celebrate marriage?

Shakespeare's comedies typically end with a wedding. However, in *Much Ado About Nothing*, it is more than just a feature of genre. When Benedick calls to Don Pedro, 'Prince, thou art sad. Get thee a wife, get thee a wife', the repeated imperative seems a genuine assertion that marriage is the ultimate source of happiness. This is conveyed through metaphor earlier in the play when Don Pedro refers to 'the new gloss' of Claudio's marriage.

Fitting the beliefs of the time, marriage is linked closely to religion. Beatrice describes her hope that Benedick will 'bind our loves up in a holy band', while Leonato says of Claudio's proposal to his daughter, 'all grace say "Amen" to it'. Marriage is also related to eternity and fidelity. When Ursula asks Hero when she is getting married, she happily replies, 'Why, every day, tomorrow!', meaning that she will be married for the rest of her life.

How do some characters criticise marriage?

Beatrice sees marriage as oppressive ('to be over-mastered … to make an account of her life') and Don Pedro notes that she 'cannot endure to hear tell of a husband'. Benedick believes that wives cannot be trusted, 'pluck off the bull's horns and set them in my forehead', and makes regular references to the traditional idea of a **cuckold**'s horns. However, both characters represent the comedy of the play and come to realise that they are wrong.

In comparison, as the villain of the play, Don John's views are never altered. When Conrade mentions Claudio and Hero's impending marriage, he sneers, 'What is he for a fool that betroths himself to unquietness?' implying a dislike for women as much as weddings.

How does Shakespeare explore infidelity?

Many of the male characters show a distrust in women's fidelity: Benedick fears being cuckolded, Claudio believes that Hero would choose other men over him, Leonato thinks his daughter capable of promiscuity the night before her marriage, and Don John knows it is a widespread suspicion that he can manipulate. Such attitudes were typical in the 16th century.

Shakespeare includes many references to infidelity, sometimes as a source of humour ('hath not the world one man but he will wear his cap with suspicion?') and sometimes drama ('Would you not swear, / All you that see her, that she were a maid, / By these exterior shows? But she is none'). When she is suspected of being 'disloyal', many insults are used against Hero: 'plague', 'rotten', 'stale', 'wanton', 'vile', 'foul', 'impious'.

Key Quotations to Learn

Benedick: 'I will do myself the right to trust none: and the fine is, for the which I may go the finer, I will live a bachelor.' (Ii)

Claudio [to Hero]: 'But you are more intemperate in your blood / Than Venus, or those pamper'd animals / That rage in savage sensuality.' (IVi)

Benedick: 'In brief, since I do purpose to marry, I will think nothing to any purpose that the world can say against it ...' (Viv)

Summary

- Although Benedick and Beatrice criticise marriage, they come to change their views.
- Marriage is linked to religion and eternity but men are suspicious of women's fidelity.
- The play ends with the assertion that marriage is the ultimate source of happiness.

Sample Analysis

One way in which marriage is celebrated is through Benedick's soliloquy, which explores his realisation that he has been wrong. His rhetorical question 'Shall quips and sentences and these paper bullets of the brain awe a man from the career of his humour?' captures his surprise that he is now thinking of marriage. The pattern of three and the 'bullets' metaphor diminish his previously negative opinions. His final words suggest the desire to be wed is natural and cannot be ignored. His words are serious but also humorous, due to the dramatic irony of the audience knowing he has been tricked by his friends.

Questions

QUICK TEST
1. What criticisms of marriage are made by Benedick and Beatrice?
2. What was traditionally used to symbolise a man whose wife had been unfaithful?
3. What does Don John's manipulation of Claudio and Don Pedro imply about men's attitudes towards women in the 16th century?

EXAM PRACTICE
Using one or more of the 'Key Quotations to Learn', write a paragraph analysing how Shakespeare presents the theme of infidelity in the play.

You must be able to: understand how Shakespeare uses the theme of noting in the play.

What is the significance of noting?

Noting is the act of closely watching, noticing and reporting things, and the characters do this throughout the play. More importantly, characters are manipulated through noting, being set up so things are heard and seen that are not what they appear.

When the play was written, 'nothing' would have been pronounced 'noting'. This creates a pun, suggesting the play is also exploring the effects ('Much Ado …') of noting.

How is noting used in a serious manner?

Noting is significant in that it is how Don John achieves his bad intentions. He discovers the plan to court Hero due to Borachio's skill at hiding himself and noting things: 'I whipped me behind the arras and there heard it'. Don John then uses noting to manipulate people, leading them to note things about Hero that are untrue.

Shakespeare emphasises noting by repeating the verb 'to hear', such as when Don John lies to Claudio, 'I heard him swear his affection', and at the wedding when Don Pedro says, 'Myself, my brother, and this grieved Count / Did see her, hear her …'

Noting creates gossip and judgements. Shakespeare uses different synonyms for talking to convey how this affects Hero. It is introduced in Don John's lines, 'I came hither to tell you … she has been too long a-talking', and continues when he lies at the wedding: 'There is not chastity enough in language / Without offence to utter them.'

How is noting used to create comedy?

The act of noting creates humour when Claudio asks Benedick if he has noticed Hero. He is hoping for approval and has a serious intent but Benedick replies, 'I noted her not, but I looked on her', implying that nothing impressed him. Shakespeare also shows Benedick noting Hero's flaws for comic purposes – the use of contrasts and parallelism in 'she's too low for a high praise, too brown for a fair praise, and too little for a great praise' is meant to annoy Claudio rather than actually criticise Hero.

The manipulation of noting is also presented as comic when it is done with good intentions, as when Benedick and Beatrice are tricked. Their eavesdropping on their friends' conversations is an act of noting. Unaware they are being manipulated, they hear things that have apparently been noted about themselves and each other. Again, synonyms for talking and listening are important to highlight the idea of noting, such as Leonato saying 'you heard my daughter tell you' and Hero claiming, 'so says the Prince and my new-trothed lord'.

Hero also foreshadows the serious side of noting that she will experience. As part of the trick, she tells Ursula she will make up a harmless lie about Beatrice to save Benedick from pointlessly loving her: 'I'll devise some honest slanders / To stain my cousin with.'

Key Quotations to Learn

Claudio: 'Benedick, didst thou note the daughter of Signior Leonato?' / Benedick: I
noted her not, but I looked on her.' (Ii)

Hero: 'One doth not know / How much an ill word may empoison liking.' (IIIi)

Friar (on why he believes Hero): '... by noting of the lady. I have mark'd / A thousand
blushing apparitions / To start in to her face ...' (IVi)

Summary

- Noting refers to how people watch, listen to and judge others.
- Shakespeare introduces the theme through Claudio noting Hero.
- The theme is used for comic effect when Benedick mocks Claudio's attraction and when the other characters trick Benedick and Beatrice into falling in love.
- Don John is used to convey the serious consequences of noting in the way that he manipulates what people see and hear in order to harm Claudio and Hero.

Sample Analysis

Noting often creates comic confusion in the play. When Antonio reports that 'much overheard by a man of mine: the Prince discovered to Claudio that he loved my niece your daughter', Leonato expects Don Pedro to woo Hero. Shakespeare often uses synonyms for talking and listening to convey the theme of noting; the verb 'overheard' links to how many of the play's events are caused by hearsay. The double meaning of 'discovered' is also effective as it relates to how characters interpret more than they should from people's speech, such as when Benedick comically searches for hidden meaning in Beatrice's words at the end of Act 2.

Questions

QUICK TEST

1. How does Claudio introduce the play's theme of noting?
2. What sort of words does Shakespeare repeat throughout the play that link to the theme of noting?
3. Who manipulates noting in order to ruin Claudio and Hero's love?
4. Who are happier victims of noting?

EXAM PRACTICE

Using one or more of the 'Key Quotations to Learn', write a paragraph analysing how Shakespeare uses the theme of noting in the play.

Secrets and Deception

You must be able to: understand how Shakespeare presents the theme of secrets and deception in the play.

How is deception linked to villainy?

Relating to the theme of noting are lying and trickery, both of which are committed by Don John and Borachio. Borachio suggests that truth and lies can be indistinguishable: 'there shall appear such seeming truth of Hero's disloyalty that jealousy shall be called assurance'.

Borachio's pride in his ability to deceive is conveyed through his use of contrasting **adverbs** 'Not honestly, my lord, but so covertly that no dishonesty shall appear in me.' He even advises Don John how to be deceptive in order to cross Don Pedro and Claudio: 'intend a kind of zeal … as in love of your brother's honour'.

Borachio boasts of his deception to Conrade, again using adverbs to highlight his abilities: 'partly by his oaths, which first possessed them, partly by the dark night, which did deceive them, but chiefly by my villainy, which did confirm any slander'. The use of verbs and parallelism also emphasises how a deception can be built up until it is believed. However, Borachio is ironically undone by secrecy as he is unaware that the watchmen are listening to the conversation.

How are secrets and deception used to create romance and comedy?

Shakespeare uses deception to create romance, particularly in Don Pedro and Claudio's plan to woo Hero at the masked ball. This scene also uses hidden identities for comedy, as when Benedick's plan to annoy Beatrice rebounds on him: 'Nor will you not tell me who you are? … Well, this was Signior Benedick that said so … he is the Prince's jester, a very dull fool.'

In the tricking of Beatrice and Benedick, both characters are deceived by their friends and family. There is a pretence of criticism, such as Don Pedro saying 'for the man, as you all know, hath a contemptible spirit', or Hero declaring, 'She cannot love … She is so self-endeared.' They also lie about the victims' secret love, claiming that Benedick 'loves Beatrice so entirely' and she 'will die if he love her not'.

Deception is also used to save Hero from shame. The friar suggests that she is 'secretly kept in' and her death announced in the hope that it will 'Change slander to remorse'. When Don John's treachery is revealed, Leonato maintains the deception in order to test Claudio's honour. He must marry a niece of Leonato's who is 'Almost the copy of my child that's dead', leading to the romantic unmasking of Hero at the end of the play.

Key Quotations to Learn

Don Pedro: 'Why, what effects of passion shows she?' / Claudio: '[Aside] Bait the hook well, this fish will bite.' (IIiii)

Beatrice: 'What fire is in mine ears? Can this be true?' (IIIi)

Borachio: 'I have deceived even your very eyes: what your wisdoms could not discover, these shallow fools have brought to light ...' (Vi)

Summary

- Secrets and deception can be used for comedy and romance, such as the tricking of Beatrice and Benedick.
- However, deception is also a sign of villainy which is portrayed through Borachio and Don John.
- Secrets and deception are used to save Hero from shame and to test Claudio's honour.

Sample Analysis

Deception is linked to evil when Borachio tells Conrade that 'the devil my master knew she was Margaret' when recounting how he and Don John have tricked Don Pedro and Claudio. He conveys Don John's malevolence by linking his superior to Satan. However, the phrase can also be interpreted as a description of Borachio's own sinfulness by implying that he sees the devil as his 'master'. He displays no shame in his words which suggests that he is proud of his abilities to deceive. This is also indicated by the verb 'knew' as it highlights the power of knowledge and how easy it is to manipulate the truth, especially when exploiting social bias such as men's distrust of women.

Questions

QUICK TEST
1. Who is proud of his abilities to deceive others?
2. According to their friends and family, what secret are Beatrice and Benedick hiding?
3. Why do Leonato and the Friar pretend that Hero has died?
4. Why does Leonato continue this deception?

EXAM PRACTICE
Using one or more of the 'Key Quotations to Learn', write a paragraph analysing how Shakespeare presents the theme of secrets and deception in the play.

Conflict, Honour and Guilt

You must be able to: understand how Shakespeare presents the themes of conflict, honour and guilt in the play.

How is conflict used in the play?

The play is set against the background of war and initially seems a comedic escape from conflict. However, it includes many individual conflicts: Benedick and Beatrice feuding; Don John setting himself against Claudio and Don Pedro; Claudio's accusations against Hero; Beatrice persuading Benedick to challenge Claudio to a duel; and Leonato's and Antonio's feelings towards Claudio and Don Pedro after Hero is shamed.

The play explores how conflict is caused by different behaviours, such as noting, deception, bias, pride and honour. Importantly, none of the conflicts have long-lasting consequences and, with the possible exception of Don John (although he is arrested at the end of the play), all of them are resolved.

Where does Shakespeare present honour in the play?

Personal and family honour are significant in the play: Leonato feels honoured to have Don Pedro stay at his home ('Please it your Grace lead on?'); Claudio has gained honour through the war and Don John is jealous of this ('hath all the glory of my overthrow'); Antonio and Leonato see Hero's possible marriage to Don Pedro as a source of honour ('we will hold it as a dream till it appear itself'); Claudio feels dishonoured when he thinks Hero has deceived him and Don Pedro feels dishonoured for having helped the courtship ('as I wooed for thee to obtain her, I will join with thee to disgrace her'); Leonato feels he and the family are dishonoured by Claudio's accusations ('Thou hast so wrong'd my innocent child and me'); and Benedick accuses Don Pedro and Claudio of lacking honour ('I must discontinue your company … you killed a sweet and innocent lady').

How does Shakespeare explore guilt in the play?

Claudio and Don Pedro both feel guilty for their mistreatment of Hero. Despite his higher status, Don Pedro pledges to undertake anything that Leonato will 'enjoin' him to do in order to 'satisfy this good old man'. However, they also point out that they were tricked, sharing the **iambic pentameter** as they make their defence: Claudio: '… yet sinn'd I not / But in mistaking.' / Don Pedro: 'By my soul, nor I'.

Interestingly, it is Borachio who seems more overwhelmed by guilt. He calls himself a villain and repeatedly asks to be executed: 'My villainy they have upon record, which I had rather seal with my death than repeat over to my shame.' He fully accepts his **culpability**, 'If you would know your wronger, look on me', and clarifies that Margaret was not part of the plot ('by my soul she was not').

Key Quotations to Learn

Don Pedro: 'I stand dishonour'd, that have gone about / To link my dear friend to a common stale.' (IVi)

Leonato: '... smirched thus, and mir'd with infamy ...' (IVi)

Borachio: '... let this Count kill me ... I desire nothing but the reward of a villain.' (Vi)

Claudio: 'Impose me to what penance your invention / Can lay upon my sin.' (Vi)

Summary

- Shakespeare includes many individual conflicts between the characters in the play but they are all resolved by the end.

- Personal and family honour are important aspects in the characters' lives and often become causes of conflict.

- Don Pedro and Claudio show guilt for their dishonourable treatment of Hero. However, Borachio arguably conveys the deepest sense of guilt for his actions.

Sample Analysis

Shakespeare uses military imagery to present the conflict between Beatrice and Benedick. Leonato light-heartedly describes 'a kind of merry war ... They never meet but there's a skirmish of wit' when speaking to the Messenger. Combining the comic genre of the play with the background of the Sicilian wars, the metaphors include contrasts to emphasise the humour in Benedick and Beatrice's antagonism. These opposites can also be interpreted as representing the notion of conflict and, in particular, the play's battle of the sexes.

Questions

QUICK TEST
1. Which characters present a comic conflict between the sexes?
2. In what different ways is the shaming of Hero linked to a loss of honour?
3. What penalty does Borachio feel he deserves?

EXAM PRACTICE
Using one or more of the 'Key Quotations to Learn', write a paragraph analysing how Shakespeare presents the theme of either honour or guilt in the play.

Tips and Assessment Objectives

You must be able to: understand how to approach the exam question and meet the requirements of the mark scheme.

Quick Tips

- You will get one question about a character or a theme. It will ask you to respond to a sho extract from the play and to link your ideas to other scenes in *Much Ado About Nothing*.
- Make sure you know what the question is asking you. Underline key words and pay particular attention to the bullet point prompts that come with the question.
- You should spend about 50 minutes on your *Much Ado About Nothing* response. Allow yourself between five and ten minutes to annotate the extract and plan your answer s there is some structure to your essay.
- All your paragraphs should contain a clear idea, a relevant reference to the play (ideal a quotation) and analysis of how Shakespeare conveys this idea. Whenever possible, you should link your comments to the play's context.
- It can sometimes help, after each paragraph, to quickly re-read the question to keep yourself focused on the exam task.
- Keep your writing concise. If you waste time 'waffling' you won't be able to include th full range of analysis and understanding that the mark scheme requires.
- It is a good idea to remember what the mark scheme is asking of you.

AO1: Understand and respond to the play (12 marks)

This is all about coming up with a range of points that match the question, supporting you ideas with references from the play and writing your essay in a mature, academic style.

Lower	Middle	Upper
The essay has some good ideas that are mostly relevant. Some quotations and references are used to support the ideas.	A clear essay that always focuses on the exam question. Quotations and references support ideas effectively. The response refers to the extract and to other points in the play.	A convincing, well-structured essay that answers the question fully. Quotations and references are well-chosen and integrated into sentences. The response covers the whole play (not everything, but ideas from the extract and a range of other Acts).

AO2: Analyse effects of Shakespeare's language, form and structure (12 marks)

You need to comment on how specific words, language techniques, sentence structures, stage directions or the narrative structure allow Shakespeare to get his ideas across to the audience. This could simply be something about a character or a larger idea he is exploring through the play. To achieve this, you will need to have learned good quotations to analyse.

Lower	Middle	Upper
Identification of some different methods used by Shakespeare to convey meaning. Some subject terminology.	Explanation of Shakespeare's different methods. Clear understanding of the effects of these methods. Accurate use of subject terminology.	Analysis of the full range of Shakespeare's methods. Thorough exploration of the effects of these methods. Accurate range of subject terminology.

AO3: Understand the relationship between the play and its contexts (6 marks)

For this part of the mark scheme, you need to show your understanding of how the characters or Shakespeare's ideas relate to when he was writing (late 1500s) or the society in which the play is set.

Lower	Middle	Upper
Some awareness of how ideas in the play link to its contexts.	References to relevant aspects of contexts show a clear understanding.	Exploration is linked to specific aspects of the play's contexts to show a detailed understanding.

AO4: Written accuracy (4 marks)

You need to use accurate vocabulary, expression, punctuation and spelling. Although it is only four marks, this could make the difference between a lower or a higher grade.

Lower	Middle	Upper
Reasonable level of accuracy. Errors do not get in the way of the essay making sense.	Good level of accuracy. Vocabulary and sentences help to keep ideas clear.	Consistent high level of accuracy. Vocabulary and sentences are used to make ideas clear and precise.

1. Read the following extract from Act 1 scene 1 and then answer the question that follows.

BEATRICE	I wonder that you will still be talking, Signior Benedick: nobody marks you.
BENEDICK	What, my dear Lady Disdain! Are you yet living?
BEATRICE	Is it possible disdain should die while she hath such meet food to feed it as Signior Benedick? Courtesy itself must convert to disdain if you come in her presence.
BENEDICK	Then is courtesy a turncoat. But it is certain I am loved of all ladies, only you excepted: and I would I could find in my heart that I had not a hard heart; for, truly, I love none.
BEATRICE	A dear happiness to women: they would else have been troubled with a pernicious suitor. I thank God and my cold blood, I am of your humour for that: I had rather hear my dog bark at a crow than a man swear he loves me.

Starting with this extract, explore how Shakespeare presents the relationship between Benedick and Beatrice. Write about:

- how Shakespeare presents the relationship between Benedick and Beatrice in this extract
- how Shakespeare presents the relationship between Benedick and Beatrice in the play as a whole.

2. Read the following extract from Act 2 scene 1 and then answer the question that follows.

DON PEDRO	And Benedick is not the unhopefullest husband that I know. Thus far can I praise him: he is of a noble strain, of approved valour, and confirmed honesty. I will teach you how to humour your cousin, that she shall fall in love with Benedick; and I, with your two helps, will so practise on Benedick that, in despite of his quick wit and his queasy stomach, he shall fall in love with Beatrice. If we can do this, Cupid is no longer an archer: his glory shall be ours, for we are the only love-gods. Go in with me, and I will tell you my drift.

Starting with this speech, how does Shakespeare present Don Pedro in the play? Write about:

- how Shakespeare presents Don Pedro in this speech
- how Shakespeare presents Don Pedro in the play as a whole.

Read the following extract from Act 4 scene 1 and then answer the question that follows.

HERO	O, God defend me! how am I beset!
	What kind of catechising call you this?
CLAUDIO	To make you answer truly to your name.
HERO	Is it not Hero? Who can blot that name
	With any just reproach?
CLAUDIO	Marry, that can Hero;
	Hero itself can blot out Hero's virtue.
	What man was he talk'd with you yesternight,
	Out at your window betwixt twelve and one?
	Now, if you are a maid, answer to this.
HERO	I talk'd with no man at that hour, my lord.
DON PEDRO	Why, then are you no maiden.
	Leonato, I am sorry you must hear: upon mine honour,
	Myself, my brother and this grieved count,
	Did see her, hear her, at that hour last night,
	Talk with a ruffian at her chamber-window;
	Who hath indeed, most like a liberal villain,
	Confess'd the vile encounters they have had
	A thousand times in secret.

Starting with this dialogue, explain how far you think Shakespeare presents Hero as a weak and innocent character. Write about:

    how Shakespeare presents Hero in this dialogue

    how Shakespeare presents Hero in the play as a whole.

. Read the following extract from Act 1 scene 3 and then answer the question that follows.

DON JOHN	I had rather be a canker in a hedge than a rose in his grace, and it better fits my blood to be disdained of all than to fashion a carriage to rob love from any: in this, though I cannot be said to be a flattering honest man, it must not be denied but I am a plain-dealing villain. I am trusted with a muzzle and enfranchised with a clog; therefore I have decreed not to sing in my cage. If I had my mouth, I would bite; if I had my liberty, I would do my liking: in the meantime, let me be that I am and seek not to alter me.
CONRADE	Can you make no use of your discontent?
DON JOHN	I make all use of it, for I use it only.

Starting with this extract, how does Shakespeare present Don John as villain? Write about:

    how Shakespeare presents Don John as villainous in this extract

    how Shakespeare presents Don John as villainous in the play as a whole.

Planning a Character Question Response

You must be able to: understand what an exam question is asking you and prepare your response.

How might an exam question on character be phrased?

A typical character question will read like this:

Read the extract from Act 1 scene 1 (from *'O my lord, when you went onward on this ended action'* to *'I would have salv'd it with a longer treatise.'*).

Starting with this extract, explore how Shakespeare presents Claudio in the play. Write about:

- how Shakespeare presents Claudio in this extract
- how Shakespeare presents Claudio in the play as a whole.   [30 marks + 4 AO4 marks]

How do I work out what to do?

The focus of this question is clear: Claudio and how his character is presented.

The extract is your starting point. What does it tell you about Claudio and how is this conveyed?

'How' is the key aspect of this question.

For AO1, you need to display a clear understanding of what Claudio is like, any ways in which he changes and where this is shown in the play.

For AO2, you need to analyse the different ways in which Shakespeare's use of language, structure and the dramatic form help to show the audience what Claudio is like. Ideally, you should include quotations that you have learnt but, if necessary, you can make a clear reference to a specific part of the play.

You also need to remember to link your comments to the play's context to achieve your AO3 marks and write accurately to pick up your four AO4 marks for spelling, punctuation and grammar.

How can I plan my essay?

You have approximately 50 minutes to write your essay.

This isn't long but you should spend the first five to ten minutes reading and annotating the extract then writing a quick plan. This will help you to focus your thoughts and produce a well-structured essay.

to come up with three or four ideas from the extract, and think about how these can developed using other parts of the play. Each of these ideas can then be written up as aragraph.

u can write your points about the extract, followed by your exploration of the rest of e play. Or you can alternate your points between the extract and the rest of the play. oose a method that best matches the question.

u can plan in whatever way you find most useful. Some students like to just make a ick list of points and then re-number them into a logical order. Spider diagrams are rticularly popular; look at the example below.

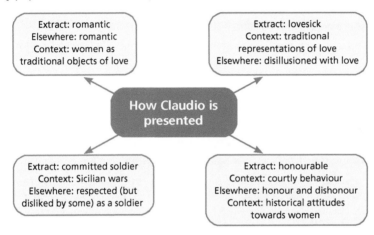

Summary

Make sure you know what the focus of the essay is.

Remember to analyse how ideas are conveyed by Shakespeare.

Try to relate your ideas to the play's social and historical context.

Questions

QUICK TEST

. What key skills do you need to show in your answer?

. What are the benefits of quickly planning your essay?

. Why is it better to have learned quotations for the exam?

XAM PRACTICE

lan a response to Question 1 from page 58.

Read the extract from Act 1 scene 1 (from *'O my lord, when you went onward on this ended action'* to *'I would have salv'd it with a longer treatise.'*).

Starting with this extract, explore how Shakespeare presents Claudio in the play. Write about:

- how Shakespeare presents Claudio in this extract
- how Shakespeare presents Claudio in the play as a whole.   [30 marks + 4 AO4 marks]

In the extract from Act 1 scene 1, Claudio is presented as a romantic character (1). 'in their rooms / Came thronging soft and delicate desires' (2). This uses the adjectives 'soft' and 'delicate' to make Claudio sound romantic (3). When Claudio speaks about Hero, he describes her looks and behaviour rather than her personality. 'how fair young Hero is'. The adjective fair means that Claudio's attraction is based on Hero's looks and the adjective 'young' means that it is based on her innocence.

This is also shown earlier in the scene. He says, 'In mine eye, she is the sweetest lady that ever I looked on.' The adjective suggests he wants someone nice and feminine and he talks about her as if she is an object. This is also shown when he uses the 'jewel' metaphor to describe her like a prize (4). Shakespeare wrote Much Ado About Nothing *towards the end of the 16th century which was a very different time to now. When the play was written, men had certain views about women and wanted a good wife (5).*

Claudio also seems romantic when he talks all lovey-dovey and like love has made him feel ill because it's given him butterflies in his tummy (6). He says, 'love's grief by his complexion!' This is saying he feels unhappy because his love hasn't been returned yet (7). This idea of love making Claudio feel bad is also in the play when he thinks Don Pedro has wooed Hero for himself. Benedick uses a simile about Claudio to mean that Claudio is unhappy. The simile is 'as melancholy as a lodge in a warren'. It means that Claudio is unhappy and it also sounds like he's lonely because Hero has gone off with Don Pedro except she hasn't really (8).

Claudio is also made to seem honourable. 'My liking might too sudden seem.' This makes him seem honourable because he wants to get Hero the proper way. This is called courtly love. The word 'seem' is important because it shows that Claudio understands it is important to have proper behaviour (9).

In other parts of the play, Claudio does not seem honourable. He seems dishonourable. This is shown by his treatment of Hero. When he decides to call her out at the wedding it is cruel. He describes her as if she is mouldy to get across that she isn't pure. He uses lots of insults that also suggest she is immoral and these are humiliating. Some of the words describe her like she is a prostitute which would be particularly bad as she is really young and innocent and of quite a high status (10).

Claudio is also a soldier and this links to how he behaves. He says, 'I look'd upon her with a soldier's eye, / That lik'd, but had a rougher task in hand / Than to drive liking to the name of love: / But now

am return'd, and that war-thoughts / Have left their places vacant'. This means that he has always
*been committed to doing his duty in the war and he has always focused his life on war rather than love
which I guess might explain why he sometimes gets things wrong about love (11).* He is young for a
celebrated soldier and Don John describes him rudely. 'young start-up hath all the glory' This is meant
*to be nasty but it also shows why Claudio makes mistakes because he is young but has risen up quickly
and is kind of not ready yet and doesn't know anything about women or how people can be liars (12).*

. The essay starts with a clear point about the extract. AO1

. A suitable quotation is selected but it would be better if this was embedded. AO1

. A technique is identified but the analysis is let down by simply repeating the point. AO2

. A stronger attempt at analysing, suggesting what specific words and images convey about Claudio. AO2

. Some context is included but it isn't fully linked to the analysis. AO3

. The expression here is too chatty, rather than academic. Always avoid slang. AO1 and AO4

. A good quotation is used, although it would be better if it had been embedded. There is some good, if a little general, analysis. AO1 and AO2

. The essay refers to another part of the play but is a little vague and some poor expression reduces the clarity. AO1 and AO4

. A new point is made clearly and is supported by evidence. There is some context and some good analysis. However, this could be explained and linked together more carefully. AO1, AO2 and AO3

0. This would be better with quotations but there are some general references to another scene in the play and the language features and their effects. AO2

1. The extract is explored further but the quotation is unnecessarily long. There is some good analysis but the writing is not academic enough. AO1, AO2 and AO4

2. The essay has some sense of conclusion with some general but effective analysis of language. AO1 and AO2

> ## Questions

EXAM PRACTICE
Choose a paragraph of this essay. Read it through a few times then try to rewrite and
improve it. You might:
- improve the sophistication of the language or the clarity of expression
- replace a reference with a quotation or use a better quotation
- ensure quotations are embedded in the sentence
- provide more detailed, or a wider range of, analysis
- use more subject terminology
- link some context to the analysis more effectively.

A proportion of the best top-band answers will be awarded Grade 8 or Grade 9. To achieve this you should aim for a sophisticated, fluent and nuanced response that displays flair and originality.

Read the extract from Act 1 scene 1 (from *'O my lord, when you went onward on this ended action'* to *'I would have salv'd it with a longer treatise.'*).

Starting with this extract, explore how Shakespeare presents Claudio in the play. Write abou

- how Shakespeare presents Claudio in this extract
- how Shakespeare presents Claudio in the play as a whole.   [30 marks + 4 AO4 mark

In the extract from Act 1 scene 1, Claudio is presented as a romantic character. Personification is used in the lines 'in their rooms / Came thronging soft and delicate desires' to convey his sudden feelings of love for Hero and how they have filled his mind (1). The verb 'thronging' suggests his surprise and this is continued by 'soft' and 'delicate' as they contrast with his life as a soldier. However, these adjectives also highlight that he welcomes his new emotions (2).

When Claudio speaks of Hero, Shakespeare uses references to her appearance and demeanour, rath than her personality. Although a modern audience may question this attitude, an Elizabethan audience would have found such representation of love familiar (3). The adjectives in 'how fair young Hero is' imply that Claudio's attraction is based on Hero's looks and innocence. This idea is established earlier in the scene where he refers to her as 'modest' and asserts that 'In mine eye, she is the sweetest lady that ever I looked on', again using adjectives to identify qualities that were traditionally seen as favourable in a wife. The repetition of references to the male gaze ('mine eye' and 'looked upon') imply that Claudio considers Hero to be a romantic object and this is emphasised when he uses a metaphor to compare her to a 'jewel' (4).

Claudio's presentation as a traditional romantic character can also be seen in how the extract presents him as lovesick (5). He comments that Don Pedro recognises 'love's grief by his complexion' and this was a traditional representation of love in the 16th century. The idea of 'grief' links to his love not yet being requited and suggests depth to his feelings (6). This is explored elsewhere when Claudio becomes disillusioned by love, believing that Don Pedro has wooed Hero for himself. Benedick uses the simile 'as melancholy as a lodge in a warren' to convey Claudio's unhappiness and to suggest the loneliness he feels without Hero (7).

Linking to the presentation of Claudio as a figure of romance, he is also characterised as being honourable. Aware of the traditional expectations of courtly love, he is worried that 'my liking might too sudden seem', and that this could be disrespectful. The verb 'seem' highlights that Claudio

nderstands the importance of proper behaviour and this is underlined soon after when he and Don
edro discuss the importance of Leonato's role in the courtship.

Vhilst he is linked to honourable behaviour elsewhere in the play, such as the Messenger's admiring
se of the verb 'borne' in his comment 'He hath borne himself beyond the promise of his age', Claudio
lso displays dishonourable behaviour in his treatment of Hero (8). His suspicions about women's
delity appear to come from social attitudes at the time and he allows these to cloud his judgement
hen he believes Don John's fabrications. His decision to 'shame her' at the wedding is cruel and
ased on feelings that his own honour has been damaged. His insults, 'She knows the heat of a
xurious bed … wanton … savage sensuality', are harsh and humiliating, and possibly display
given the men's earlier jokes about brothels) a hypocritical disgust for female sexuality (9).

ome of the contradictions and flaws in Claudio's character, such as his apparent trust of any man over
woman, may be linked to his life as a soldier (10). The play is set against the backdrop of Sicilian wars
nd the metaphor describing his mind being full of 'war-thoughts' conveys his commitment to duty; the
ct that he has so far focused his life on war, the 'rougher task in hand', rather than love may explain
is less favourable behaviour. Shakespeare shows that this commitment has gained him praise as well
s jealous hatred. Don John describes Claudio as a 'young start-up [who] hath all the glory', but this
lso captures the naivety that Claudio displays throughout the play, something that is later voiced by
ntonio who repeatedly calls him a 'boy' for his mistreatment of Hero (11).

- The opening sentences establish a clear point about what Claudio is like in the extract, along with an embedded quotation as evidence. AO1
- Shakespeare's use of language to convey meaning is analysed in detail. AO2
- Specific context is used to enhance analysis. AO3
- Several points from elsewhere in the play are explored, with consistent analysis of language. AO1 and AO2
- The extract is returned to, establishing another way in which Claudio is presented. AO1
- An embedded quotation is followed by language analysis. Specific context is used to enhance the analysis. AO1, AO2, AO3
- Another point from elsewhere in the play is explored through analysis of language. AO1 and AO2
- Contrasts are used to add depth to the exploration of Claudio's character. AO1
- Vocabulary is used with precision and there is a high level of accuracy throughout. AO4
0. The final point about Claudio also creates a sense of summary and conclusion. AO1
1. There continues to be a range of analysis. AO2

Questions

EXAM PRACTICE
Spend 50 minutes writing an answer to Question 1 from page 58.
Remember to use the plan you have already prepared.

Possible Theme Questions

1. Read the following extract from Act 2 scene 1 and then answer the question that follows

ANTONIO	[To HERO] Well, niece, I trust you will be ruled by your father.
BEATRICE	Yes, faith, it is my cousin's duty to make curtsy and say 'Father, as it please you.' But yet for all that, cousin, let him be a handsome fellow, or else make another curtsy and say 'Father, as it please me.'
LEONATO	Well, niece, I hope to see you one day fitted with a husband.
BEATRICE	Not till God make men of some other metal than earth. Would it not grieve a woman to be overmastered with a piece of valiant dust? To make an account of her life to a clod of wayward marl?
	No, uncle, I'll none: Adam's sons are my brethren; and, truly, I hold it a sin to match in my kindred.
LEONATO	[To HERO] Daughter, remember what I told you: if the Prince do solicit you in that kind, you know your answer.

Starting with this extract, how does Shakespeare present ideas about marriage in the play?
Write about:

- how Shakespeare presents ideas about marriage in this extract
- how Shakespeare presents ideas about marriage in the play as a whole.

2. Read the following extract from Act 3 scene 3 and then answer the question that follows.

BORACHIO	... I have tonight wooed Margaret, the Lady Hero's gentlewoman, by the name of Hero. She leans me out at her mistress' chamber-window, bids me a thousand times good night. I tell this tale vilely. I should first tell thee how the Prince, Claudio and my master, planted and placed and possessed by my master Don John, saw afar off in the orchard this amiable encounter.
CONRADE	And thought they Margaret was Hero?
BORACHIO	Two of them did, the Prince and Claudio; but the devil my master knew she was Margaret; and partly by his oaths, which first possessed them, partly by the dark night, which did deceive them, but chiefly by my villainy, which did confirm any slander that Don John had made, away went Claudio enraged ...

Starting with this conversation, explore how Shakespeare presents the theme of deception.
Write about:

- how Shakespeare presents the theme of deception in this conversation
- how Shakespeare presents the theme of deception in the play as a whole.

Read the following extract from Act 3 scene 1 and then answer the question that follows.

| URSULA | [Aside] She's limed, I warrant you: we have caught her, madam. |
| HERO | [Aside] If it proves so, then loving goes by haps: Some Cupid kills with arrows, some with traps. |

Exeunt HERO and URSULA

BEATRICE	[Coming forward] What fire is in mine ears? Can this be true?
	Stand I condemn'd for pride and scorn so much?
	Contempt, farewell! And maiden pride, adieu!
	No glory lives behind the back of such.
	And, Benedick, love on; I will requite thee,
	Taming my wild heart to thy loving hand:
	If thou dost love, my kindness shall incite thee
	To bind our loves up in a holy band;
	For others say thou dost deserve, and I
	Believe it better than reportingly.

Starting with this extract, how does Shakespeare present attitudes towards love? Write about:

  how Shakespeare presents attitudes towards love in this extract

  how Shakespeare presents attitudes towards love in the play as a whole.

Read the following extract from Act 1 scene 1 and then answer the question that follows.

BENEDICK	... for, truly, I love none.
BEATRICE	A dear happiness to women: they would else have been troubled with a pernicious suitor. I thank God and my cold blood, I am of your humour for that: I had rather hear my dog bark at a crow than a man swear he loves me.
BENEDICK	God keep your ladyship still in that mind! so some gentleman or other shall 'scape a predestinate scratched face.
BEATRICE	Scratching could not make it worse, an 'twere such a face as yours were.
BENEDICK	Well, you are a rare parrot-teacher.
BEATRICE	A bird of my tongue is better than a beast of yours.
BENEDICK	I would my horse had the speed of your tongue, and so good a continuer. But keep your way, i' God's name; I have done.
BEATRICE	You always end with a jade's trick: I know you of old.

Starting with this dialogue, explore how Shakespeare presents conflict. Write about:

  how Shakespeare presents conflict in this dialogue

  how Shakespeare presents conflict in the play as a whole.

Planning a Theme Question Response

You must be able to: understand what an exam question is asking you and prepare your response.

How might an exam question on theme be phrased?

A typical theme question will read like this:

Read the extract from Act 1 scene 1 (from *'Thou wast ever an obstinate heretic'* to *'hang me up at the door of a brothel-house for sign of a blind Cupid'*).

Starting with this extract, explore how Shakespeare presents the theme of infidelity in the play. Write about:

- how Shakespeare presents infidelity in this extract
- how Shakespeare presents infidelity in the play as a whole.   [30 marks + 4 AO4 marks]

How do I work out what to do?

The focus of this question is clear: infidelity.

The extract is your starting point. Who is talking about infidelity, who do they think lacks fidelity, and what is their opinion of it?

'How' is the key aspect of this question.

For AO1, you need to display a clear understanding of what characters think about infidelity, who they suspect of infidelity and where this is shown in the play.

For AO2, you need to analyse the different ways in which Shakespeare's use of language, structure and the dramatic form help to explore infidelity. Ideally, you should include quotations that you have learnt but, if necessary, you can make a clear reference to a specific part of the play.

You also need to remember to link your comments to the play's context to achieve your AO3 marks and write accurately to pick up your four AO4 marks for spelling, punctuation and grammar.

How can I plan my essay?

You have approximately 50 minutes to write your essay.

This isn't long but you should spend the first five to ten minutes reading and annotating the extract then writing a quick plan. This will help you to focus your thoughts and produce a well-structured essay.

Try to come up with three or four ideas from the extract, and think how these can be developed using other parts of the play. Each of these ideas can then be written up as a paragraph.

You can write your points about the extract, followed by your exploration of the rest of the play. Or you can alternate your points between the extract and the rest of the play. Choose a method that best matches the question.

You can plan in whatever way you find most useful. Some students like to just make a quick list of points and then re-number them into a logical order. Spider diagrams are particularly popular; look at the example below.

Extract: even the most beautiful women capable of infidelity according to Benedick
Context: gender in 16th century
Elsewhere: despite being a figure of innocence, Hero is accused of infidelity

Extract: infidelity is a source of humiliation
Context: traditional horn imagery
Elsewhere: infidelity is a source of dishonour
Context: soldiers and honour

How infidelity is presented

Extract: women cannot be trusted
Context: gender in 16th century
Elsewhere: it is the men who cannot be trusted or relied upon
Context: subversion of 16th-century attitudes

Summary

- Make sure you know what the focus of the essay is.
- Remember to analyse how ideas are conveyed by Shakespeare.
- Try to relate your ideas to the play's social and historical context.

Questions

QUICK TEST
1. What key skills do you need to show in your answer?
2. What are the benefits of quickly planning your essay?
3. Why is it better to have learned quotations for the exam?

EXAM PRACTICE
Plan a response to Question 1 from page 66.

Grade 5 Annotated Response

Read the extract from Act 1 scene 1 (from *'Thou wast ever an obstinate heretic'* to *'hang me up at the door of a brothel-house for the sign of blind Cupid.'*).

Starting with this extract, explore how Shakespeare presents the theme of infidelity in the play. Write about:

- how Shakespeare presents infidelity in this extract
- how Shakespeare presents infidelity in the play as a whole.   [30 marks + 4 AO4 marks]

In the extract, Shakespeare establishes the idea that although men found women attractive they did not trust them (1). This links to the time when the play was written (2), and it is presented by how Don Pedro describes Benedick in the extract. 'an obstinate heretic in the despite of beauty' (3). He uses the noun 'beauty' to suggest that Benedick will not even trust the most attractive women because he thinks their looks are a deception (4).

This is also seen when Hero is accused of infidelity. Claudio shames her at the wedding by accusing her in front of everyone at the wedding. Being accused of infidelity would have been humiliating but this suggests that men were always suspicious that a woman might commit infidelity (5). Claudio repeats ideas that Hero is not as she seems, claiming that she looks innocent and pure but is really an immoral woman who commits infidelity. One way this is conveyed is through classical imagery and similes (6). All of this shows that they had double standards for men and women in the 16th century (7).

Infidelity is also explored in the extract by explaining the men's attitudes because they are linked to not wanting to be humiliated. Benedick uses a metaphor, 'a recheat winded in my forehead'. A 'recheat' was a horn so this is a reference to the horn which was supposed to be a symbol for a cuckold when a woman cheated on her husband. It shows that men didn't want to be made a fool of by women so were suspicious of their possible infidelity (8).

This is also seen when infidelity is linked to a loss of reputation for men. The men are soldiers so their honour and reputation were very important to them, especially in the 16th century when society had a lot more traditional values and expectations. This is felt by Don Pedro when he says, 'I stand dishonour'd, that have gone about / To link my dear friend to a common stale.' The word 'dishonour'd' suggests he has been harmed simply by association (9). It's like infidelity is catching or something and the men are scared of getting it. Although this is a dumb idea, it explains why the men react to Hero's infidelity likes it's really evil and sinning (10).

Shakespeare plays around with the idea the men have that women cannot be trusted. In the extract, Benedick says, 'I will do myself the right to trust none.' This means that he doesn't believe that women are not always infidelity. It is also shown by the word 'right' which means he really believes he's right (11). However, in Much Ado About Nothing, *it is men who cannot be trusted: Don John* and Borachio are liars and Claudio and Don Pedro are horrid to Hero. Even though Don John is *called a 'bastard' they believe him more than Hero which is probably because she is a woman. When *the truth is revealed Claudio is shocked (12).*

1. The opening sentence establishes a point but it could be linked more clearly to the theme of infidelity. AO1

2. Some contextual understanding is implied but it is not explained clearly enough. AO3

3. A good quotation is used as evidence but it would be better if it was embedded within a sentence. AO1

4. Although the word 'heretic' could be explored, there is some good analysis of the quotation. AO2

5. The essay moves beyond the extract to develop the point but becomes description rather than analysis. Repetitive language shows a lack of sophistication and precision. AO1 and AO4

6. There is a suitable reference to the play but a quotation would have allowed more analysis. The reference to classical images and similes is good but undeveloped. AO2

7. There is an attempt to link analysis to context but it is rather vague. AO3

8. A new point is established, a quotation is partially embedded and there is some successful analysis of language. AO1 and AO2

9. Although it could be expressed more effectively and some terminology could be included, there is some good analysis and attempts are made to link it to clear context. AO1, AO2 and AO3

10. The vocabulary here is unsophisticated; a more academic style is needed. AO4

11. There is some successful analysis, although the language is imprecise and too informal. AO1, AO2 and AO4

12. There is some sense of a conclusion but it could be phrased more effectively and linked more carefully to the theme of infidelity. AO1

Questions

EXAM PRACTICE
Choose a paragraph of this essay. Read it through a few times then try to rewrite and improve it. You might:

- improve the sophistication of the language or the clarity of expression
- replace a reference with a quotation or use a better quotation
- ensure quotations are embedded in the sentence
- provide more detailed, or a wider range of, analysis
- use more subject terminology
- link some context to the analysis more effectively.

Grade 7+ Annotated Response

A proportion of the best top-band answers will be awarded Grade 8 or Grade 9. To achieve this you should aim for a sophisticated, fluent and nuanced response that displays flair and originality.

Read the extract from Act 1 scene 1 (from *'Thou wast ever an obstinate heretic'* to *'hang me up at the door of a brothel-house for the sign of blind Cupid.'*).

Starting with this extract, explore how Shakespeare presents the theme of infidelity in the play. Write about:

- how Shakespeare presents infidelity in this extract
- how Shakespeare presents infidelity in the play as a whole.   [30 marks + 4 AO4 mark

Shakespeare appears to question the perception that women were prone to infidelity (1). This false notion is seen throughout the play, suggesting it was a typical male attitude in the 16th century (2) and it is presented by Benedick in the extract. Don Pedro describes his friend as 'an obstinate hereti in the despite of beauty', accusing him of distrusting even the most attractive women. The use of religious language in 'heretic' implies that Benedick will not put his faith in a female and sees their 'beauty' as a deception (3).

*These attitudes are also seen when Hero is accused of infidelity. Claudio uses the similes 'You seem to me as Dian in her orb, / As chaste as is the bud ere it be blown' to assert that she hides her true nature (4). The classical imagery refers to the goddess of chastity while the natural imagery depicts an untouched flower to suggest virginity. However, he contrasts both these images by then linking what he sees as her true infidelity to 'Venus' and 'animals that rage in savage sensuality', creating an impression of disgust that is heightened by the **sibilance**. These ideas are emphasised later in the scene through parallelism when Hero is described as 'most foul, most fair' and 'pure impiety and impious purity' to convey how her beauty masked her immorality. Linking to the double standards for men and women at the time, her apparent act of infidelity is linked to sin, shame and ultimately death, whereas the man (Borachio in disguise) is simply called a 'ruffian' (5).*

The men's attitude to infidelity is explained in the extract when, through the traditional imagery of horns, it is linked to humiliation (6). Benedick uses the metaphor of having 'a recheat winded in my forehead' to suggest his wariness of wearing the proverbial cuckold's horn. He continues these references with his description of having to 'hang my bugle in an invisible baldrick' to emphasise the male fear of being emasculated by a woman (7). Elsewhere in the play, infidelity is linked to a loss of reputation for the male. This is felt by Don Pedro when he says, 'I stand dishonour'd, that have gone about / To link my dear friend to a common stale', with the verb 'dishonour'd' suggesting he has bee harmed simply by association. Referring to Hero as a prostitute shows, again, the sense of disgust that the men have for infidelity and could also imply that she is seen as being like a venereal disease that can affect others. This is supported by Don John's words, 'O plague right well prevented', when he convinces the men of Hero's immorality (8).

Ultimately, Shakespeare subverts the belief that women cannot be trusted. This 16th-century misogyny is apparent in Benedick's words from the extract, 'I will do myself the right to trust none', where he implies that he doubts the fidelity of all women. His conviction in this perception is indicated through the double meaning of 'right'. However, in Much Ado About Nothing, *from Don John and Borachio's villainous deceptions to Claudio and Don Pedro's wilful cruelty towards innocent Hero, it is actually the men who lack fidelity (9). Despite his past hostility, Don John's word is believed above that of Hero, primarily because she is a woman. When the truth is revealed, Claudio's metaphor, 'I have drunk poison whiles he utter'd it', conveys his horror that his preconceptions around fidelity have led to the death of the woman he loved (10).*

1. The opening sentence establishes a clear point about infidelity. AO1
2. Context is used to enhance the exploration. AO3
3. An embedded quotation is followed by analysis of language and structure. AO1 and AO2
4. The essay moves beyond the extract to develop the point. AO1
5. Detailed analysis of language and patterns of imagery, related to context. AO2 and AO3
6. The extract is returned to, alongside specific context, in order to establish another way in which infidelity is explored. AO1 and AO3
7. Again, an embedded quotation is followed by language analysis. AO1 and AO2
8. Ideas are developed by moving beyond the extract and analysing language in detail. AO1 and AO2
9. Context is used to illuminate the analysis. This section is typical of how sophisticated vocabulary has been used with precision. AO2, AO3 and AO4
10. A sense of conclusion is created in the final sentences. There is a high level of accuracy throughout. AO1 and AO4

Questions

EXAM PRACTICE
Spend 50 minutes writing an answer to Question 1 from page 66.
Remember to use the plan you have already prepared.

Glossary

Abstract noun – a noun that is an idea or quality rather than a concrete object.

Adjective – a word that gives more information about a noun.

Adverb – a word that gives more information about a verb.

Alliteration – a series of words beginning with the same sound.

Aside – a piece of dialogue that is performed as if some, or all, of the other characters on stage cannot hear it.

Bawdy – dealing with sexual matters in a comic way.

Benevolence – kindness.

Classical – related to the myths and legends of ancient Greece and Rome.

Conventional – what is generally, or traditionally, done and believed.

Courtly – polite and respectable behaviour linked to people of status.

Cuckold – a man whose wife has been unfaithful.

Culpability – guilt.

Dramatic irony – a technique whereby the audience knows something that a character on stage does not know.

Duel – a fight between two people, often with swords, to settle a matter of honour.

Enjambment – when a sentence of verse continues onto a new line without being interrupted by punctuation.

Epitaph – words written about someone who has died (for example, to be inscribed on a tombstone or read at a funeral).

Escapism – a way to be distracted from reality and to imagine another life somewhere else.

Euphemism – substituting a milder word or phrase for one that might have seemed too harsh or rude.

Foreshadow – to indicate, or warn about, a future event.

Hyperbole – use of exaggeration to emphasise an idea.

Iambic pentameter – the rhythm of an unstressed beat followed by a stressed beat, repeated five times in a line.

Illegitimacy – when a child is born out of wedlock.

Imagery – words used to create a picture in the imagination.

Infidelity – the act of being unfaithful.

Irony – using language in a way that suggests the opposite meaning of the words actually used.

Malapropism – using a similar-sounding but incorrect word instead of the one intended.

Metaphor – a descriptive technique, using comparison to say one thing is something else.

Naive – innocent or showing a lack of experience and judgement.

Noun – a naming word for a person, place, animal or object.

Ominous – threatening.

Parallelism – using the same pattern of words in a sentence or phrase for effect.

Patriarchal – relating to a society ruled by men.

Pattern of three – three related ideas, placed together for emphasis.

Personification – writing about an object, place or idea as if it has human characteristics.

Presumptuous – moving beyond the limits of what is expected or acceptable.

romiscuous – having many sexual relationships.

ronoun – a word that takes the place of a oun (such as: I, she, it).

un – using a word that has a double meaning n order to create humour; a word that can e substituted for a similar-sounding word to reate additional meaning.

uatrain – a four-line stanza of poetry.

econciled – to have good relations restored.

epartee – a conversation that contains quick, vitty comments and replies.

epetition – saying a word or phrase more han once for effect.

equite – to return something (often love).

hetorical question – a question asked in rder to create thought rather than to get a pecific answer.

ite – a ceremony.

hrewish – bad-tempered, bossy, aggressive usually describing a woman).

Sibilance – repetition of s sounds for effect.

Simile – a descriptive technique, saying one thing is 'like' or 'as' another.

Sin – an immoral act.

Soliloquy – a speech performed alone on stage (or that other characters present cannot hear) to reveal what a character is thinking.

Stichomythia – when characters speak alternate lines of dialogue, each time repeating or developing a word or image from the previous speaker's line.

Subvert – undermine an established thought or system.

Traditional – long established or old fashioned.

Verb – a word that expresses an action or state of being.

Verb phrase – a group of words making up a verb.

Woo – to try to gain someone's love.

Wordplay – using different meanings, innuendo and ambiguities in words, often to create humour.

Answers

Pages 4–5

Quick Test

1. Because Claudio has fought well in the war.
2. Beatrice ('I wonder that you will still be talking …')
3. They have been reconciled.
4. Benedick mocks Claudio and tries to dissuade him; Don Pedro encourages Claudio and offers to help him.

Exam Practice

Analysis might include: Beatrice's religious exclamation to suggest that being friends with Benedick is like a sin; her use of the **verb** 'caught' to imply he is like a disease; her implication that he uses other people's money; Benedick's combination of politeness ('dear Lady') and insult ('Disdain'); his question jokingly implies that he wishes she was dead.

Pages 6–7

Quick Test

1. Antonio mistakenly believes that Don Pedro is in love with Hero. The audience already knows that he is only planning to woo her on Claudio's behalf.
2. Because he is illegitimate.
3. Don John dislikes Claudio. He is jealous of his position with Don Pedro, thinks he is too young to have received such honour and calls him presumptuous for planning to woo Hero.
4. He has a negative view of marriage and calls it 'unquietness'.

Exam Practice

Analysis might include: the repeated references to unhappiness to convey his general demeanour; the verb phrase 'cannot hide' to suggest he refuses to pretend to be nicer than he is; the repetition of 'if I had' to emphasise that he feels restricted; the verb 'bite' implies he has a vicious nature; he is unromantic and sexist, seeing a lover as a 'fool' and marriage as 'unquietness'.

Pages 8–9

Quick Test

1. That he is unhappy and unfriendly.
2. He expects Hero to be wooed by Don Pedro.
3. Masked, he tries to annoy Beatrice but the joke rebounds when she describes her low opinion of him.
4. He is angry and upset.

Exam Practice

Analysis might include: love is presented as being competitive and something that can ruin friendships (the use of 'constant … Save in'); love is linked to unity and harmony through the use of **parallelism** and **pronouns** ('you are mine, I am yours'); love is presented as a mutual sacrifice ('give away myself … exchange'); metaphors convey a comic side to love through Don Pedro's plan to unite Benedick and Beatrice, although this also implies that love is stronger than anything else and everyone can fall in love.

Pages 10–11

Quick Test

1. Don John must tell Claudio and Don Pedro that Hero is unfaithful. At night, he should then take them to where they can see Hero's bedroom window. In disguise, Borachio will speak to Margaret as if she is Hero and Borachio her lover.
2. Because Claudio has previously mocked others who have fallen in love.
3. That she is unable to admit her true feelings.
4. He realises that he is in love with Beatrice.

Exam Practice

Analysis might include: the noun 'fool' shows that Benedick is dismissive of romance and lovers; the verb 'railed' describes his negative attitude to love but the reference to appetite and the verb 'alter' convey how he realises his love for Beatrice; the humorous contrasts (die/live, bachelor/married) emphasise how he has changed his opinion of love.

Pages 12–13

Quick Test

1. Dramatic irony
2. Beatrice would mock Benedick for loving her; she would continually make jokes about it to Hero; it is pointless as Beatrice would only find fault with him anyway.
3. They think he is going to admit his love for Beatrice.
4. They will both shame her at the wedding.

Exam Practice

Analysis might include: deception is presented as humorous and good-natured using the metaphor 'false sweet bait', and this is emphasised by the dramatic irony of the situation, with Beatrice thinking she is spying on them; the use of hyperbole in the simile and in the images of lovesickness exaggerate the situation to make the deception seem humorous; the use of metaphor has a double meaning ('plague' refers to Hero's apparent infidelity but also relates to Don John's wish to destroy everyone's happiness) that conveys a more serious and cruel image of deception.

Pages 14–15

Quick Test

1. Dogberry's speech features malapropisms: he misuses vocabulary (often more sophisticated words), resulting in it having the opposite meaning to what he intends.
2. Borachio and Don John
3. She pretends she has a cold.
4. An ominous tone

Exam Practice

Analysis might include: Margaret uses double meaning to create bawdy humour – the word 'stuffed' is meant as an adjective for having a cold and as a verb for having had sexual intercourse; the use of question and answer creates humorous repartee, with Beatrice's witty reply suggesting that Margaret isn't very clever or funny ('not seen enough'); Dogberry confuses 'comprehended' with 'apprehended' and 'aspicious' (auspicious) with 'suspicious', as well as repeating and contradicting himself (promising 'one word' that turns into many).

es 16–17

ck Test

They think he is joking.

He appears to be pleased and to think she deserves it.

He feels she has brought shame upon herself and the family.

She says it will be a sign of his love for her.

m Practice

alysis might include: Claudio is disgusted by what he believes er promiscuity ('the heat of a luxurious bed') and uses a trast to convey his anger at her deceiving him; Leonato's taphor shows his own disgust at Hero and that she will never rid of the shame; the Friar's adjectives ('sweet', 'guiltless') vey his trust in Hero and this is emphasised by the metaphor ing error' to imply she is a victim.

es 18–19

ck Test

He now believes that she has been falsely accused.

They are shocked, feel guilty and offer to make amends.

Leonato's niece / Antonio's daughter

Love sonnets written about each other.

m Practice

alysis might include: grief and anger are conveyed by nato's belief that no father has suffered as he has, and is emphasised by the verbs 'lov'd' and 'overwhelm'd'; tonio's metaphor 'slander'd to death' shows his grief and er; Don Pedro's simile and Claudio's metaphor suggest ir horror at the truth, and the realisation of what they ve done, by comparing it to something painful and deadly ering them; although their love is mostly performed for nour, the reference to their 'hearts' implies the depth of trice and Benedick's love.

es 20–21

ck Test

To create escapism. The sunny, warm atmosphere would also match the themes of comedy and romance.

She is submissive to men and Shakespeare demonstrates her inferior position by not allocating her many lines of dialogue.

She is not submissive to men and mocks them.

This is a slang term for being illegitimate.

m Practice

alysis might include: Antonio and Leonato expect Hero to ow their wishes with regard to marriage (they think she is be wooed by Don Pedro and this would increase their social tus); Hero's silence implies that she wishes to submit to their wishes; trice mocks this idea of a woman's duty and suggests t, if Hero doesn't find him attractive, she should choose neone else; Beatrice implies that she would never marry ause she is superior to any man and wouldn't want to have ubmit to him.

es 22–23

ck Test

The acceptance of social hierarchies, **traditional** gender roles and the importance of marriage

The ending restores order. This means that any subversion of social conventions is, ultimately, not radical or threatening.

The use of nothing/noting can suggest the play is about the consequences of making judgements based merely on appearance or gossip; the use of thing/nothing can suggest that the play is all about men's desire for women and how this causes many problems.

Exam Practice

Analysis might include: despite the social importance of marriage, Beatrice never wants to marry; she uses a religious image ('blessing') for not getting married, despite marriage being a holy ceremony; she also jokes about dressing a man as her lady-in-waiting to emphasise the idea that men are inferior to her.

Pages 24–25

Quick Test

1. A speech, performed alone on stage or unheard by other characters, that reveals a character's feelings.

2. Act 2 scene 3 and Act 3 scene 1

3. Problems are resolved, Claudio and Hero get married (and Beatrice and Benedick plan to marry) and there is a dance.

Exam Practice

Analysis might include: Dogberry's six accusations against Borachio and Conrade are the same, deliberately making his speech unnecessarily long; the order of his speech doesn't make sense because he calls his third point 'secondarily', his fourth point 'sixth, and lastly,' and his fifth point 'thirdly'; Don Pedro then deliberately mirrors this confused order in his own speech to mock Dogberry; Claudio adds a joke (the sarcasm in 'rightly reasoned') about Don Pedro successfully mimicking Dogberry's confused speech ('in his own division').

Pages 26–27

Quick Test

1. She is rude to him and mocks him.

2. That men are inferior to women and none are good enough for her.

3. Don Pedro. It highlights that her comments should come across as light and witty rather than harsh and shrewish.

4. Once she is tricked into realising her love for Benedick, she tries to hide her emotions but her friends know what she is feeling.

Exam Practice

Analysis might include: Beatrice's use of military **imagery** to mock Benedick as stupid, describe her conflict with him and give her opinion that she always gets the better of him; use of stichomythia as she responds to his question by repeating his words ('disdain'), using a food metaphor to turn it against him and suggest he has no qualities to talk positively about; 'mirth' and 'no matter' remind the audience that Beatrice is a fun character in a comedy, and these important words are emphasised in her speech through the **alliteration**; use of animal imagery ('taming') and the **verb** 'requite' to show her realisation of her love for Benedick.

Pages 28–29

Quick Test

1. Dismissive

2. To amuse his friends.

3. Unaware she is speaking to him at the masked ball, she describes her low opinion of him.

4. As well as their early insults towards each other, they are both tricked by their friends, both try to hide their lovesickness and both are mocked by their friends who know their true feelings.

Exam Practice

Analysis might include: the adjective 'disdain' and the rhetorical question in response to Beatrice show Benedick's quick-wittedness; he uses hyperbole to exaggerate his dismissive attitude to marriage in order to amuse his friends; the verb 'misused' shows he is upset by Beatrice's words about him and

Answers   77

feels he is a better person than she considers him to be; the contrast between 'requited' and 'railed' conveys his change of opinion about marriage and this is emphasised by the reference to food ('appetite alter'), while the rhetorical questions suggest he is surprised or confused by his new feelings.

Pages 30–31
Quick Test
1. The accusation against Hero.
2. She asks him to kill Claudio. At first he refuses but then accepts when she says it would be a sign of his love.
3. They joke about not actually loving each other and just marrying out of pity.

Exam Practice

Analysis might include: Beatrice manipulates his words (she repeats his use of 'love' and refers to how he has sworn his feelings for her when she uses the verb 'swearing') to convince him to kill Claudio as a sign of his commitment to her; the mix of romantic ('love') and unromantic ('suffer', 'against', 'in spite of') language suggests their unwillingness to truly admit their feelings; their love is represented by the paired pronouns ('Thou and I') and the alliteration ('too wise to woo'), as well as acknowledgement of their shared characteristic (neither behaves 'peaceably').

Pages 32–33
Quick Test
1. Silence or obedience, virtue and beauty
2. She does not have many lines so her character is conveyed through the opinions of others (most notably, Claudio).
3. She is more talkative, perceptive, confident, funny and mischievous.
4. Forgiveness and virginity

Exam Practice

Analysis might include: Claudio's metaphor suggests Hero is beautiful and that she surpasses others but it also relates to how she is treated as an object; Beatrice makes three references to Hero's obedience but, although there is a tone of mockery, she is criticising social conventions rather than Hero herself; Hero's Cupid imagery displays her witty and confident side when amongst women as she enjoys playing a trick on Beatrice (and a sense of mischief is emphasised by the speech being an aside); the phrase 'maiden modesty' conveys Hero's innocence as well as her role as a victim and the importance of her virgin status (its importance is also implied through the use of alliteration to emphasise the two words).

Pages 34–35
Quick Test
1. Her looks and his conventional expectations of women.
2. He doesn't want to wait a few days to get married.
3. Don John fools him twice: convincing him that Don Pedro is wooing Hero for himself, and then making him believe that Hero has been unfaithful.
4. He admits guilt in his treatment of Hero, compares it to sin, offers to undertake any punishment that Leonato decides and readily accepts marrying the niece he has never met.

Exam Practice

Analysis might include: the superlative adjective 'sweetest' shows his love for Hero but this is based on her appearance and behaviour, rather than her personality, and the references to 'eye'/'looked' emphasise this; the personification of time as too slow conveys his loving eagerness to get married but could also imply he is rash and impatient; the adjectives 'bashful'

and 'comely', alongside the comparison to a brother and sister, convey how honourably he has behaved in the courting of Hero; the use of contrasts emphasises his anger at being deceived by Hero, while the negative adjectives and nouns depict his disgust at her apparent immoral behaviour.

Pages 36–37
Quick Test
1. He is addressed respectfully, such as liege, Grace and Highness.
2. He approves and helps with the courtship.
3. Benedick
4. He feels he has lost honour because he encouraged and helped Claudio to woo Hero.

Exam Practice

Analysis might include: Leonato's use of the phrase 'your Grace' shows Don Pedro's status as Prince of Aragon, as well as implying that he is highly respected, but Don Pedro is also respectful to people in return (offering to go inside 'together' rather than taking the 'lead'); the adjective 'worthy' shows he approves of Hero and encourages Claudio, proving himself to be more romantic than Benedick; the 'net' metaphor (and the use of the aside) display Don Pedro's comic, mischievous side and this is emphasised by the noun 'sport'.

Pages 38–39
Quick Test
1. He accepts Beatrice's unconventional attitudes to men and marriage, and jokes with her. However, he expects his daughter to obey him when he thinks Don Pedro is going to propose.
2. He displays forgiveness (first when he thinks Claudio has taken Hero's virginity and then when Claudio apologises for slandering her); despite Claudio being a young soldier, he challenges him to a duel to uphold the family honour.
3. He believes Don Pedro and Claudio over his own daughter (presumably because they are men) and wishes Hero dead because of the shame he thinks she has brought on the family.

Exam Practice

Analysis might include: Leonato displays traditional patriarchal values when using language of ownership and exchange in relation to the wedding, but is also very happy about the union linking it to his Catholic religion; the reference to death sounds cruel and judgemental but his attitude towards family shame would have been more recognisable to a 16th-century audience; the verbs 'prove' and 'dare' show his honour and bravery in challenging Claudio to a duel, while his list of sarcastic insults conveys his anger.

Pages 40–41
Quick Test
1. He is miserable.
2. He resents that Claudio is closer to his brother than he is himself. He also suggests Claudio is too young to have achieved such honour, thinks him presumptuous for wanting to marry Hero and dislikes his happiness.
3. He flees rather than accept the consequences (but is apprehended).
4. Borachio

Exam Practice

Analysis might include: the cage metaphor suggests he feels socially trapped due to being the illegitimate brother and his refusal to 'sing' means that he will not try to be happy); the linking of the verbs 'cross' and 'bless' suggest his immorality and that he only gains happiness from others' unhappiness, as well as indicating his jealousy of Claudio's place by Don Pedro's side; the pattern of three nouns (relating to obstacles) shows his determination to cause trouble, while linking them to the word 'medicinable' shows that other people's unhappiness makes him happier; the **abstract noun** 'wickedness' refers to Hero but reflects his own malevolent nature and his willingness to lie and deceive.

Pages 42–43

Quick Test

1. They are lower-class, comic characters.
2. To appear more intelligent or superior, and to match what he sees as the status of his job.
3. Because he is foolish but honest.
4. Beatrice

Exam Practice

Analysis might include: Dogberry's malapropism (mistaking 'tolerable' for 'intolerable') makes him appear comically foolish, as does his criticism of people who 'babble', given his tendency for over-long, rambling speech; he wants Conrade punished for calling him an 'ass' (donkey/idiot) but makes himself look a fool by comically repeating the insult as if it is something he agrees with (the comedy is highlighted by him contrasting showing off his status by using imperatives or orders).

Pages 44–45

Quick Test

1. She is modest, quiet and submissive.
2. Honour and strength
3. Subvert
4. He thinks they lack fidelity and are unfaithful to their husbands.

Exam Practice

Analysis might include: the verb 'ruled' links to how women were expected to obey their fathers; Don Pedro talks about courtship as if it is a competition and about Hero as if she is a prize or object ('won'), although he praises Beatrice despite her negative comments about men and marriage; the use of parallelism and matching language indicates that men and women are more similar than Benedick and Beatrice, and perhaps the audience, think.

Pages 46–47

Quick Test

1. Love was often linked to pain, illness or grief until it was requited.
2. The development of a relationship, characterised by rules of etiquette and by the man earning the woman's love.
3. By killing Claudio.
4. Pride

Exam Practice

Analysis might include: while love is linked to emotion (the verb 'feel'), it is also linked to suitability and how well a woman conforms to social expectations (the adjective 'worthy'); the rhetorical question conveys Benedick's surprise at Beatrice falling in love while the verb 'must' indicates that

her love is too powerful for him to resist; love is linked to illness ('sick') but also the fun of matchmaking (the Cupid metaphor); Beatrice acknowledges that personal 'pride' and 'contempt' for social expectations have been an obstacle to her falling in love.

Pages 48–49

Quick Test

1. Beatrice suggests that marriage is oppressive and Benedick appears to believe that wives are not faithful.
2. Horns
3. That men did not trust women and found it easy to believe they would be unfaithful.

Exam Practice

Analysis might include: the verb phrase 'trust none' implies that Benedick doesn't trust any women and this is emphasised by the double meaning of the word 'right' (he also uses wordplay with 'fine'/'finer' to suggest that the only penalty of not trusting women is never getting married and that this is a better way to live one's life); Claudio uses the adjective 'intemperate' to suggest Hero cannot be trusted, followed by **classical** imagery and animal imagery to suggest that she has followed an instinct for desire and been unfaithful.

Pages 50–51

Quick Test

1. He asks Benedick if he has noted Hero.
2. Synonyms for 'seeing' and 'hearing'
3. Don John
4. Benedick and Beatrice.

Exam Practice

Analysis might include: Claudio shows the amorous side of noting while Benedick shows the humorous side, using the double meaning of 'noted' to suggest that nothing impressed him about Hero; Hero's metaphor foreshadows how she will become a victim of noting through Don John's manipulation of Claudio and Don Pedro; noting can also have a positive effect, such as where the Friar believes Hero's innocence after observing her reactions at the wedding (using a metaphor for the horror on her face).

Pages 52–53

Quick Test

1. Borachio
2. Their love for each other.
3. They hope that Claudio, and more widely the people of Messina, will feel sorry for her death and forget her shame.
4. To test Claudio's honour.

Exam Practice

Analysis might include: the noun 'passion', as used in relation to Beatrice, is a fabrication, while a fishing metaphor is used to describe deceiving Benedick (emphasised by it being performed as an aside); the metaphor describes the pleasant shock of the deception when Beatrice hears about Benedick's love for her, and this is emphasised by the rhetorical question (which has a comic effect due to the dramatic irony of the audience knowing it is not 'true'); Borachio may sound proud in these lines but actually he is feeling guilty; the use of the abstract noun 'wisdoms' implies that anyone can be deceived, while Shakespeare may be using traditional imagery of truth and light (implying goodness) to indicate that deception is evil.

Pages 54–55

Quick Test

1. Beatrice and Benedick
2. Claudio feels dishonoured for having been deceived by her; Don Pedro feels dishonoured for having helped Claudio to woo her; Leonato feels she has dishonoured the family's reputation; Leonato and Antonio later feel that Claudio and Don Pedro have dishonoured their family's reputation because of how they treated Hero; Benedick says that Claudio and Don Pedro have acted dishonourably towards her.
3. Death

Exam Practice

Analysis might include: Don Pedro uses the adjective 'dishonour'd' to suggest that his reputation and sense of pride have been damaged because he helped Claudio to woo someone deceptive and immoral (emphasised by the contrasting of the noun phrases 'dear friend' and 'common stale'); Leonato's fears that the family's honour has been harmed are conveyed through the repetition of words linking to dirt ('smirched', 'mir'd') and the use of the abstract noun 'infamy'; Borachio's guilt is displayed in his request for death, saying it is the only 'reward' he deserves, and referring to himself as a 'villain'; Claudio's guilt is conveyed through religious language, referring to his treatment of Hero as a 'sin' and offering to do any 'penance' (make a recompense).

Pages 60–61

Quick Test

1. Understanding of the whole text, specific analysis and terminology, awareness of the relevance of context, a well-structured essay and accurate writing.
2. Planning focuses your thoughts and allows you to produce a well-structured essay.
3. Quotations give you more opportunities to include specific AO2 analysis.

Exam Practice

Ideas might include: the insults that they direct at each other and how this continues elsewhere in the play; their mutual dislike of love and how this changes later in the play once they are tricked by their friends; the use of comedy in this scene to present a 'merry war' between them and how this changes after the more serious events at Hero's wedding.

Pages 64–65 and 72–73

Exam Practice

Use the mark scheme below to self-assess your strengths and weaknesses. Work up from the bottom, putting a tick by things you have fully accomplished, a ½ by skills that are in place but need securing, and underlining areas that need particular development. The estimated grade boundaries are included so you can assess your progress towards your target grade.

Grade	AO1 (12 marks)	AO2 (12 marks)	AO3 (6 marks)	AO4 (4 marks)
6–7+	A convincing, well-structured essay that answers the question fully. Quotations and references are well-chosen and integrated into sentences. The response covers the whole play.	Analysis of the full range of Shakespeare's methods. Thorough exploration of the effects of these methods. Accurate range of subject terminology.	Exploration is linked to specific aspects of the play's contexts to show detailed understanding.	Consistent high level of accuracy. Vocabulary and sentences are used to make ideas clear and precise.
4–5	A clear essay that always focuses on the exam question. Quotations and references support ideas effectively. The response refers to different points in the play.	Explanation of Shakespeare's different methods. Clear understanding of the effects of these methods. Accurate use of subject terminology.	References to relevant aspects of context show a clear understanding.	Good level of accuracy. Vocabulary and sentences help to keep ideas clear.
2–3	The essay has some good ideas that are mostly relevant. Some quotations and references are used to support the ideas.	Identification of some different methods used by Shakespeare to convey meaning. Some subject terminology.	Some awareness of how ideas in the play link to its context.	Reasonable level of accuracy. Errors do not get in the way of the essay making sense.

Pages 68–69

Quick Test

1. Understanding of the whole text, specific analysis and terminology, awareness of the relevance of context, a well-structured essay and accurate writing.
2. Planning focuses your thoughts and allows you to produce a well-structured essay.
3. Quotations give you more opportunities to include specific AO2 analysis.

Exam Practice

Ideas might include: the way Antonio and Leonato display traditional patriarchal attitudes towards marriage when speaking to Hero, and how this is shown again when the marriage to Claudio is approved; Beatrice's criticism of these traditional values and how this changes by the end of the play; Beatrice's view that marriage is oppressive and how she is later tricked into changing her opinion, seeing pride as something that was an obstacle to marriage; Beatrice's negative view of marriage differing from Benedick's negative view of marriage.